Introduction

"Do not seek love, but the barriers to love wi

In 1981 after their betrothal, Lady Dianna Spencer and Prir
reporter if they were in love, to which Prince Charles replie
Prince Charles graciously did not ask the reporter to define
criticized for being honest in confessing to his ignorance of what being *"in love"* means.

The challenge is identified by the following diagram of eight ancient Greek philosophical perspectives against which we might compare our limited experience of love. However, if we are unable to explain what we are unable to define, we may never discover how much unexplored love has fallen through our fingers, and I recall the wisdom of Marcus Aurelius,

"It is not dying, but living that men should fear"

This book has been written to try to understand the complexity and mystery of love from the finest philosophical minds, and theologians of our history. To do this, I have selected a verse for us to consider from Shakespeare, (without doubt our greatest writer) and a single Biblical text from the Apostle John, (without doubt one of the most influential witnesses of the Christian faith). These verses expose the size of our challenge in understanding the mystery of enduring love. It also sets the bar against which we may courageously measure our own lives, because as Socrates wisely said, *"an unexamined life is not worth living,"* but if we are afraid to look at ourselves, what does this reveal about us? As we explore the following thoughts of truly great men, we will begin to discover what the following verses mean.

"Love is not love that alters, when it alteration finds," (Shakespeare, Sonnet 116)

The following is a glimpse into the logic and imagination of some of the finest minds of our history which I have borrowed from the philosophers of ancient Greece and Biblical theologians, all of which are beautiful love stories of reconciliation. The Greek philosophers were the greatest thinkers in history, and Biblical scholars the most profound. More has been written about love in the Bible than any book ever published. As we explore the following thoughts of truly great men, we will discover what love is.

"If we do not love, we can never know God, because God is love." (1 John 4:8)

Love is the most profound philosophical and theological challenge ever addressed by the cleverest people in human history. We are humbled, and emotionally challenged, when we capture the thoughts of truly great minds, revealed in a line of a poem, or a Biblical text, which moves our hearts.

Our failure to understand being "in love" is because we do not understand love, for which we have one tiny four-letter word, which attempts to explain an infinite range of emotional and physical challenges, but in reality, explains very little. The following quotations and diagram reveal the extremely rich, life-changing tapestry available for us to teach and share.

(Rumi) "You are not a drop in an ocean, you are an ocean in a drop."
(Socrates) "Educating the mind without educating the heart is no education at all."
(Thomas Aquinas) "What we love, reveals who we are."
(Plato) "Being loved gives you strength, loving gives you courage."
Aristotle) "Knowing yourself is the beginning of wisdom."

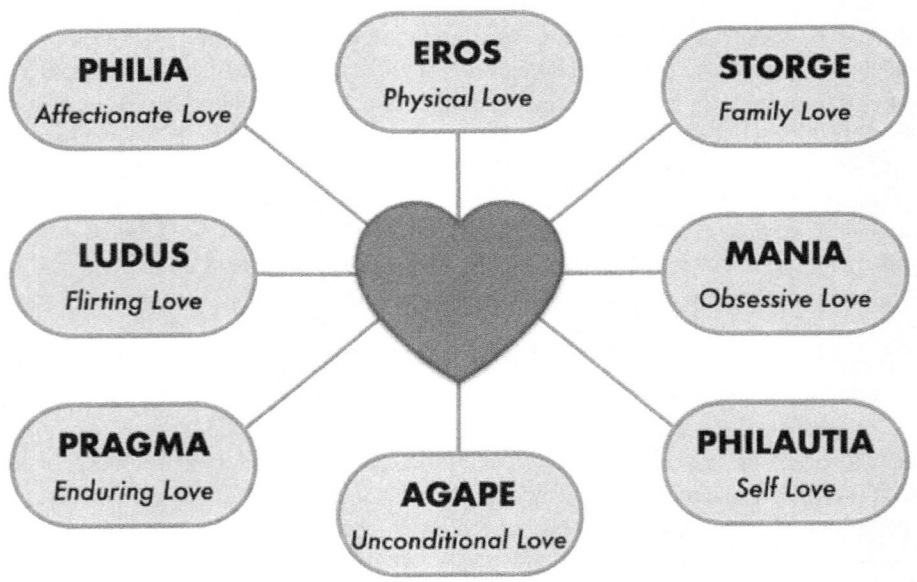

Chapter 1
ENERGY

"Everything is energy, if you match the frequency to the reality, you cannot help but obtain that reality, it can be no other way, it is not philosophy, it is physics." (Albert Einstein)

As we will have noted from the diagram drawn together by embracing the consolidated wisdom of the Bible and philosophers of ancient Greece, there are many ways in which most people might discover and experience one of the single disconnected dimensions of love.

However, as the diagram indicates there are far more ways to experience love than we may be aware of. This is often at the expense of falling to capture more than one single perspective of this very complex experience, or settling for less than is always available, if the code to love can be discovered. The code is simple, but the price of acquisition is high, because it involves recklessly abandoning the pursuit of all self-interest and focusing our loving energy upon the subject of our love, which strategy will rapidly build a congruous frequency of energy between us.

Einstein's opinion is understandably scientific but, simplified, it means that before the relationships begin, the energies of both parties must achieve congruous frequencies, or similar wave lengths of energy. This allows both parties to immerge from cold isolation into the warmth of a single, more powerful, bilateral energy of two united entities. This symbiotic phenomenon is validated by Aristotle, who wisely said:

"The whole is greater than the sum of the parts."

However, Einstein's view is also foreign to what the Bible teaches, which contradicts science and tells us that whilst science can be taught, love cannot be taught, because it is a spiritual phenomenon which can only be learned, when first experienced by the beneficiary of loving energy. The Biblical view is validated by Christian marriage, where one plus one does not make two, it makes a much larger number, because there is a spiritual and physical merging of two committed souls, with comparable frequencies of energy.

After becoming aware we were first unconditionally loved by our loving parents, we learned of love by observing the power of their love for us. If a child is not loved during their early formative years, the child may never discover or enjoy what love is, because it is impossible to know, or understand what has never been seen or experienced, as the Bible quietly tells us:

"We love because we learned of love by being first loved" (1 John 4:19)

The question this raises, which we should perhaps first address, is this: Is love a physical or spiritual experience, or is it both, or perhaps very much more.? To answer this very difficult question we should first consult the view of another leading scientist Sigmund Freud, the Austrian neurologist, and father of psychoanalysis.

After a lifetime studying human behavior, Freud taught that human life ran on tension and pleasure, and for Freud it had little to do with love. Spiritual love is an instinctive and spontaneous experience of united congruous frequencies of energy, because while sex can be organized, love is utterly illogical and cannot be intellectually programmed or organized. Freud defined this tension not as love, but as a physical product of sexual libido, or energy being built up within the body, and his solution to this tension, was not making love, it was a sexual release, or discharge of this powerful energy.

However, masquerading as a spiritual experience, so called physical love or sex can be organized, because it is often used as a currency and traded between couples and countries as a commodity, in the world's oldest profession, where love seldom exists. It is not possible to fully capture love until we fully understand that love at its most pure is a spiritual phenomenon in which sex may play no part.

After an untold number of years circa 500 BC of attempting to define the purest love, which is unconditional, the word chosen by the theologians and consensus of wise men of Greece was, "Agape" This great word became the consolidated opinion of the great men of the day, relating first to human relationships, but primarily to the relationship between God and each of us as individuals. Agape is one of the most powerfully eloquent words in any language, which we will deal with more fully in the last chapter of this book.

Agape defines a spiritual experience captured by abandoning self-interest, and recklessly focusing our hearts and prayerful energies on enlarging the interests of the subject of our love. Abandoning self-interest guarantees our reckless unconditional love will be strengthened, reciprocated and returned to us.

This is our distant target, because it is a largely unexplored dimension of spiritual love, which we all as infants possessed at its most pure and is an entirely spiritual experience freely available to us and is entirely without conditions. However, at a human level this is very difficult to understand and experience because human agreements are driven by self-interest, to which many subtle conditions of controlling a relationship are often attached.

The only way we can experience unconditional or Agape spiritual love, is to first discover if we are able to recklessly abandon our own self-interest and find a frequency which connects us to God in partnership. We are then able to seek God for an Agape experience, a secret protected by its incomprehensibility, because spiritual love cannot be taught; it can only be learned by an intimate relationship with God, and our neighbor, by our personal faith.

If your desire is to experience spiritual love you must reflect upon a time when you have sensed God in your life, because this will not be the first time God has tried to contact you to discover the experience before you can begin to develop it, with a potential partner.

After this first epiphany, we will begin to feel a movement of subtle energy, in a warming of feelings towards God, and to us from God, which will become the essential basis of all other dimensions of love that we will, in due course, capture and embrace. We will also be preparing our hearts to love comprehensively at the highest human level, which is the target of this book. Through the scriptures, we pass energy back to our partnership with God in prayer, but some of this powerful re-circulating energy will remain and slowly build within us and begin to re-shape our lives, and all our relationships.

At this point, our lives begin to change, as we adopt a new frequency of sensitivity to the Holy Spirit, and we will never be the same again because we will attract, and be attracted to, a very different frequency of energy. Our faith will have created access to an ocean of grace which if captured by us will change our lives and understanding of love forever.

Agape is the unconditional dimension of spiritual love, which often arrives as an epiphany and it is why there are over one billion Christians in the world enjoying an intimate frequency in a unique personal relationship with God, where other than the responsibility of reciprocating the love we receive, there are no conditions.

If love comes as a physical experience, it could easily masquerade as a spiritual one, which needs no matching frequency to simply download energy, but may possess the illusion of logical entitlement managed by the mind, and not the heart of a participant. However, one grey day, two plus two no longer makes four, and the logically assembled pieces of love fall apart and cannot be re-assembled, because the spiritual super-glue was counterfeited.

If, however, our union is forged spiritually, first with God and the many dimensions of love, it automatically becomes fused together with the mysterious spiritual super-glue, which for Christians is the Holy Spirit. This makes separation of the parts impossible, because love is massively greater and more secure if experienced with God than in any passing dramatic human physical encounter.

Our relationship with God does not mean all our prayers will be answered, but it does mean that our lives will never be the same again, and we will experience an epiphany as millions of other spiritual minded men and women have done, though the ages. This profoundly moving experience will provide remarkable insight into the hearts and minds of people we meet, with insight and oversight of the remaining perspectives of love in our diagram. This is due to energy released in loving and being loved unconditionally, and it will open our love life to a new and unimaginable experience, and if there is better news than this for humankind, I for one, have never heard it.

If you will be patient with me for just one moment. I would like to lower our perspective from the lofty heights of theology, to where the rubber hits the road.

I would like to illustrate this phenomenon from the perspectives of theology and physics. However, even if you avoided these esoteric subjects at school, I would be grateful if you could be a little patient with me, just for a moment while I explain, and we will swiftly pass by.

The secret of Christianity is that we can only begin to understand and love God, when we retrospectively examine our lives and become aware of how long, and how much, God, has loved us, and by grace protected us, *(I John 4:19).*

The vital principle here is that our love can only begin as a reaction to first being loved by God, and spiritually this would be a bilateral experience with God who loved us first, even before we were in diapers and likely to be unlovable.

At this point there commences a flow and contra-flow of loving energy between us, in the form of our prayers to God, and returned to us through the poetry of Scripture. I am reminded again of the great scientist, commenting on wave lengths of energy, which I am repeating, but I feel it will be clearer by a metaphorical image, because much of Scripture is taught pictorially by metaphor and parable. The number eight is the symbol of infinity, because spiritually it implies continuity, and has no beginning or end, with the energy of the grace of God flowing down to us, to be reciprocated by our returning that energy back in our prayers, *as* Albert Einstein, *says:*

> *"Everything is energy, if you match the frequency to the reality, you cannot help but obtain that reality, it can be no other way, it is not philosophy it is physics."*

After trying to apply this philosophy to commercial, legal, or political opportunities, I decided to look more closely at emotional intelligence and neurolinguistics, (the languages of the heart and nervous system), of the people I encountered in important meetings. My objective was to create a Biblical atmosphere of reciprocal good will, of flow and contra-flow of benevolent energy, because I have always believed that anger breeds anger, just as love breeds love.

Therefore, accepting the advice of Einstein, balancing frequencies of energy with the people I was meeting might make them more sympathetic to my proposals, which at times involved advising on the transfer of serious sums of money on behalf of the British Government.

My plan was to spend a little time before an important meeting endeavoring to calm myself and benevolently visualize the person I was meeting to be someone of very high quality, which individual character research has been much easier for me, since the advent of social media. Emotional intelligence helped me understand empathy and to think with my heart, but with neurolinguistics, I was amazed how much confidential information is given away in body language.

Love is a proper response to a perception of value, because it is impossible and illogical not to love the quality we sense in other human beings; everyone has some quality and if we look long enough, we will find the evidence of human value. The curious consequence is that just as aggression breeds aggression so love breeds love, and harmony breeds harmony.

I have been in meetings where personal relationships developed quickly or were irreversibly lost because of incompatible frequencies. Golf should be the classic model, because the frequencies in golf could not be more congruous or powerful, and many successful people play golf. It appears everyone has secret second interests, and if this secret can be discovered, and the frequencies of the common interest captured, it becomes a first interest, and the game is over, before it is even played.

Christian theology teaches us about faith and faithfulness, stating that without faith it is impossible to please God *(Hebrews 11:6).* This faith inspires over a billion Christians to experience and sustain an, "In love" reciprocating relationship with God, every day. It is remarkable evidence of a flow and contra flow, exchanging love for love, or being in love.

This, of course reminds us of Einstein's theory, of matching frequencies of energy, but he fails to see that, with Christians, the powerful additional resource of energy is the super-glue effect of the person and work of the Holy Spirit.

We have all experienced meeting someone new, and knowing immediately whether we are comfortable in developing the acquaintance or moving on. The frequencies will either become stronger, balanced, or repelled, and I would like to share with you one of my many happy memories of shared energy, which powerfully validates the empathy and raw power of spiritual union, or balanced frequencies.

Some time ago I travelled to southern California to meet an important Vietnamese politician and businessman, who was vital to a project in which I had a serious interest. He was a small, dapper man looking down at me from behind a large desk, and I felt a little intimidated, which at this early stage in our relationship was not what I wanted to feel. However, I had suspected that our meeting might be difficult because, based on the history of English history in Asia, cutting English businessmen down to size before important meetings was not an uncommon sport in some Eastern countries.

However, looking past him, I saw on the wall a framed incomprehensible motivational quotation, written, I presumed, in the Vietnamese language but with a small Biblical text that I could identify, in the bottom corner of the picture. It was Genesis 15:1 which I immediately recognized and I recited to him, in English.

"Fear not Abraham, I am your shield, and exceeding great reward" (KJV Genesis 15:1)

He jumped up, smiling. "You speak my language?" he enquired. "No," I said, "but I am familiar with that Biblical text, which has been translated into many languages."

He came quickly around his desk and, after hugging me, we recognized in each other the love of Scripture bonding deeply in the frequency of energy we instantly shared. Our united energy transcended our independent financial self-interests, and after successfully concluding our business, he told me the most remarkable story I have ever heard, regarding finding faith.

On the day the United States abandoned Vietnam, the army of the north swept down and occupied the town where he was studying Law. He was taken with hundreds of other undergraduate students to a political prison camp in the north, for special political education where his daily, non-academic, responsibility was cleaning the ditch, which ran from the officer's toilets to a stream below the camp.

As prisoner, students were not allowed reading material, so he would daily wash a soiled newspaper, dry it in the sun, and share it with fellow prisoners, until one day he noticed the print and paper were of higher quality, and he realized that the prison officers were using Bible pages as toilet tissue. His friend and several prisoners came to faith, through reading surviving pages from the Bible, one of which was the Biblical text on the wall of his office.

This is a perfect model of creating human relationships, because, after finding what appears to be desirable target for our love, we should endeavor to match the frequency of energy between us, which means we will find happiness, but only if we can match and balance the natural phenomenon of the frequency of our energies, because they may not unite without adjustment, concession or influence.

The challenge we have is failing to define what we are unable to explain, because we are thinking and talking about the greatest spectrum of spiritual, physical, emotional, and intellectual possibilities known to humankind. We can love, or be loved every day of our life, but never experience being, "In love". Why not? The answer is simple, but universally misunderstood.

The ancient Greek philosophers had many words to describe different aspects of love, which we will be examining. Love is a jigsaw puzzle of many aspects of the human emotional and physical experience, most of which we may never understand because unless our love is fearless, unconditional, and reckless, it is not love, it is some form of emotional imbalance.

Love is powerful inexplicable spiritual energy, and being in love is a diagram of a figure of eight two-way street, symbolic of infinity and continuous flow of energy travelling from opposing directions, and constantly reciprocating, uniting and energizing hungry open hearts whenever the energies cross, they merge, if only for the briefest moment.

Chapter 2

WEAPONIZED LOVE

"The only love we keep is the love we give away" (Aristotle)

Being in love is a continuous exchange of spiritual benevolent energy which will slowly die unless regularly renewed by exchange of comparable reciprocal messages of the heart. Being in love demands a flow and contra flow of spiritual energy between two open hearts where self-interest is abandoned, and both lives are enlarged.

A fundamental prerequisite for the integrity of a sustainable spiritual relationship is faith, and faithfulness, because even if infidelity is only an occasional passing thought, it will diffuse and destroy any hope of an enduring relationship. I will never forget, many years ago, on the eve of my wedding while in my early twenties, my mother who was poorly uneducated but a very wise Bible student and a strong puritanical lady, put her hand on my shoulder, and said to me

"If this young girl is not enough for you my lad, twenty girls will not be too many"

While I was sad with the apparent lack of confidence my mother appeared to have in me, I came to see that she understood me much better than I understood myself, as most mothers do. Bilateral relationships are secure and essential for two lovers but will never work if three people are in a relationship. The structure is defective and will collapse under the first strain.

A two-person partnership may also be compared to a joint bank account into which both partners deposit their monthly income but draw out only living expenses, leaving a little surplus money undisturbed to accumulate. This inevitably means every four weeks their joint spiritual and emotional reserves become larger. Their love becomes deeper and more enduring, due to the financial security they are creating without which there can be no emotional security.

It is the reckless exchange of spiritual energy between lovers which is the greatest joy, of being in love, and I am reminded of a line on loving exchange, from a poem by Sir Phillip Sydney, a contemporary of William Shakespeare, indicating that the secret experience of being in love has been here for very many years, and is readily available for every generation:

"I know this heart, for once it was my own, by just exchange, one for another given, there never was a better bargain driven."

Being in love must always involve the balance of generous exchange by putting more on the scales than is taken off, because when generosity is weaponized, it will melt the heart of the most selfish partner and increase your own emotional reserves.

We also must be aware of the very great danger to a relationship of failing to manage a basic family budget and running out of cash. Financial problems often provoke self-interest and anxiety followed by the "blame game" which is the cause of a breakdown in many otherwise excellent relationships.

The great secret of love is that it is a bilateral partnership into which benevolent energy is invested by two entities on a continuous basis. However, in the case of a spiritual partnership with God, the highest form of love will have been when discovering matching frequencies with the super-glue of the Holy Spirit. However, the same rules of careful maintenance apply because loving energy is either growing or dying directly proportionate to the energy individually invested, as spiritual energy feeds upon itself, or dies by neglecting itself.

The enemy of achieving the highest form of love is self-interest, because if we are preoccupied with ourselves, only a part of us is available for building our partner. Conversely if we invest our energy in our partner, the energy will symbiotically grow, beautifully, and exponentially, enlarging our partner and in consequence it will eventually, like a figure of eight, flow back to ourselves. The additional legacy we have created will be ours to enjoy together, and we begin to learn, the only way to change our partner is to love them, because when love is weaponized, it is indefensible.

Being in love for someone in the Christian faith may be a multi-lateral spiritual experience, because on special holy days like Christmas, millions of people are simultaneously communicating with God. This involves a massive flow and contra-flow of benevolent energy with prayers to God and answers from God, through prayer and the poetry of scripture. Theologically this puts all Christian communicants in the same ocean of grace, and the same matching frequency, which maintains a state of being in spiritually consummated love, which is a truly remarkable and memorable experience and is best memorialized by the following:

"An unexamined life is not worth living" (Socrates)

Being in love is the greatest spiritual experience available for humankind, because in loving we are connected to every other lover and from whom, by the grace of God, we draw energy. Perhaps the questions we should be addressing is, why are we not enjoying the positive and powerful experience of being in love today, and how it is possible we have allowed this greatest of all life's opportunities, to slip through our fingers?

The question we should perhaps address is, can we recover or discover love before it is too late? The answer is no, if our perception of love is impeded by self-interest, and we are not prepared to put more on the scales than we take off, being in love is not an experience we will ever enjoy.

If we asked any group of people what being, "In love" means, we would have many different answers, which is curious because philosophers and theologians have been discussing this blessed state for thousands of years, and yet curiously we remain blissfully ignorant, and fail to succeed in pursuing and capturing, the experiences of love, which is always on offer to us. As we consider these questions, the most important realization to accept is that the creation of an enduring happy life is a matter of our individual personal choice. This applies equally to loving, being loved, or being in love; they are all a matter of personal choice.

This unique insight was captured by John Donne, one of our greatest metaphysical poets and writer on matters of love, less fashionable perhaps than William Shakespeare. but certainly comparable. Donne wrote the following line regarding our range of choices, in a 16th century poem, indicating that our choices are often far too painful to discuss, defer, or deny:

"Be your own palace, or the world will be your jail"

What Donne is saying, is that the quality of our life is our responsibility, but the challenge we have is that we do not see the world as it is, we see the world as we are, because the world is a mirror and can only reflect what it sees. If we are suffering from low self-esteem or for any reason we become depressed, the world around us will also appear depressed. if we are angry the world will appear angry in response to the emotional posture we choose to adopt. While anger will always return anger, so love will always return love, and the palace of our greatness identified by John Donne, is always waiting for us to occupy, although based on our previous experience and mistakes, we may choose isolation and jail, but always be proud and secure in the position you now hold, and always remember the advice of Pythagoras:

"Above all, respect yourself"

Respecting ourselves must involve recognizing the value we modestly see in ourselves, juxtaposed to the value we see in others, and loving what we see. Love is a logical response to a perception of value. Perhaps loving a new-born child, a flower, sunset, or quality in another human being to whom we are physically or emotionally attracted. Love must be a response to a perception of quality, because not loving value, or quality, is illogical.

To understand being in love, we must first understand with what or whom are we in love, and to do this we will be examining the thoughts of very different philosophers and theologians, who met over thousands of years ago in their symposiums and churches. These great minds debated for long periods, often for a generation, over just one aspect of the jigsaw puzzle of love, which wisdom they are bequeathing to us today.

However, we will never understand or experience being "In love" until we have abandoned perhaps years of self-interest, and met someone in whom we see exceptional value, and which value we would like to acquire for ourselves.

It is here the mystery of being "In love" begins, not intellectually but as a tender growing plant, when we feel benevolent energy flowing from us to the subject of our admiration and benevolent energy flowing back to us in greater volume, as a figure of eight, from another open heart. It is one of the most explosive moments of our lives.

If perchance the subject of our interest also sees value in us, we will become aware of the greatest miracle and secret ever hidden from humankind. This the creation of an additional third entity, equally as powerful and wonderful as when two people physically create a new child. It is the simple equation of one plus one equaling one, and not two, because the new entity created by the energy of love is massively greater than the sum of the two individual parts. We will experience a flow and contra-flow of spiritual energy between our own heart and the heart of the person to whom we are attracted. This is dynamic and will either become more powerful or it will begin to die, as like all tender growing plants, enduring love must be constantly nurtured.

Throughout history, spiritual leaders have shared their faith and confessed to experiencing an epiphany which changed their lives, because whilst spiritual energy cannot be proven, there is massive irrefutable evidence of this experience changing lives. The curious phenomenon does not often occur in collective assemblies, because it is an intensely personal and intimate spiritual experience, often occurring when an individual is feeling lost and needs fellowship. However, while sitting in the back of a church, or searching for someone with whom to share their life, they find faith in God, which offers to them by meditation another entity with whom they can intimately communicate by faith; it is a win, win exercise. The world has hundreds of thousands of monasteries, colleges, and places of worship with millions of scholars searching to understand the phenomena of faith, where they can love and be loved by God, who they cannot see, or physically embrace.

The incomprehensible consequence of this is, the more we focus our loving energy and meditate, the more loving energy flows towards us, and from us. Although the prayers of the supplicant may not be answered in precisely the way they want, the supplicant's life will begin to change, and I am reminded of an old Jewish proverb:

"If you want to make God laugh, tell Him your plans"

Coming to faith, is a simple personal decision which immediately puts God into the center of our life and with whom we can share and grow a sacred personal fellowship in a flow and contra-flow of benevolent spiritual energy. This exchange is the consequence of God opening a spiritual path of faith between Himself and us. However, notwithstanding the value to us of studying the eight totally different aspects of the Greek philosophers' phenomena of love, we will be comparing the contrasts with what the Bible teaches, which we cannot ignore, because for thousands of years the Bible has been the only secure route to the secrets of love.

What we are able achieve in matters of our faith, we can also achieve in our career and human relationships because the more we invest in our spiritual lives, the greater will be our physical experience because spiritual empathy is the super-glue of love and unity, which binds our hearts and minds together.

The Apostle Paul teaches in his letter to the Ephesians, chapter 2, verse 8, that our reconciliation to God is not due to our efforts; Paul tells us we are saved by grace through faith, due entirely to the unconditional love of God who is waiting to hear from us. The net result of this vital knowledge is as soon as we became aware God has fallen in love with us, we fall in love with Him, and the flow and contra-flow of energy begins, as the Apostle John reminds us.

Ever since the Christian faith began over two thousand years ago, scholars have been trying to understand the biblical theology of "God is Love" by capturing God's values and applying them to their own lives. The consequence of loving God as He has loved us creates a powerful flow of benevolent energy flowing between God and humankind. Spiritual growth is acquired by the merging of two open hearts, and no matter how wise or clever we might be, nothing of value can be sustainably achieved if we are living a life of emotionally self-interested isolation. However, before we begin this challenge, we might look at the kind of person who may never experience love in the many dimensions in which it was meant to be enjoyed.

There are two fundamental principles involved, the first is that love cannot exist where self-interest is present, because the delicate flower of reckless love will never bloom in the soil of selfishness. The second principle is that love will die if isolated because it must unite with a comparable inward and outward flow of Spiritual energy to survive, expand, and flower. If we are considering a permanent partnership, any residual selfishness retained by either party must be abandoned early in the relationship, or the fragile seeds of true love will never see the sunlight or be discovered. This is because both partners will instinctively know something important is missing and hidden or disguised self-interest is often the cause.

The pattern is often similar, when two people meet and with comparable frequencies recognize certain qualities in each other, and it is a natural human reaction to admire and perhaps fall in love with those qualities, which we may desire for ourselves and hope one day to acquire. However, take care, as Geoffrey Chaucer wisely wrote in his Canterbury Tales in, 1345, two hundred years before William Shakespeare:

"Love is blind and cannot see"

This most profound philosophy of Geoffrey Chaucer was copied and adopted by Shakespeare in two of his plays, namely the Two Gentlemen of Verona, and the Merchant of Venice, revealing that the deeper the attraction of love, the greater the degree of blindness and loss of sight. Unfortunately, what we miss may appear insignificant in early meetings, but may become progressively more significant, exposing structural defects in the relationship.

I once asked a friend I was counselling to list the qualities of the lady he was proposing to divorce, when he first fell in love with her. This he did and I subsequently suggested he ignored any newly acquired characteristics and re-visit those early qualities, and fall in love with her again, building on her specific qualities, and ignoring what was missing. He produced a note of his wife's qualities, and it became clear to me he was still in love with her. While he was able to build on his wife's values which are there, he will never build on what is not there, unless or until he takes the trouble to put them there. However, I am pleased to say he accepted that history may repeat itself because his new lady would not be perfect, and he was reconciled to his wife, who generously accepted much of the responsibility for the failure of their marriage. I reminded him of the profound wisdom of Marcus Aurelius, which is the greatest motivational advice I have ever heard, but most people ignore:

"Do not dream for what you do not have, reflect on what you do have"

You may ask, what about the millions of people living alone, where is the bilateral opportunity for fellowship? I would respond by saying that being in love is an entirely spiritual experience and does not need to be intellectually or physically validated, because God will always speak to us in love through the Scriptures, and we can always speak to God in prayer. It is bilateral, energy must flow both ways, which needs at least two entities to transmit and receive. It was John Donne, who captured this most profound philosophical and theological truth during one of the most profound statements ever made, by anyone:

"No man is an Island of itself, every man is a part of a continent"

The heart is a jig-saw puzzle with many pieces, none of which appear to contain anything of value in isolation. However, we are aware from the beautiful picture on the cover of a puzzle, that while one piece of the picture may be ugly, or misshapen in isolation and mean very little, that one piece may have a massive influence on the final picture when assembled, when one small piece may mean everything. Everyone has an opinion of love, and some experience, good, bad, or indifference and many will have experience of lost love, and grieve the loss, because grief is the price, we pay for loving unconditionally, as Alfred Lord Tennyson reminds us:

"It is better to have loved and lost, than never to have loved at all"

However, the important question we need to address is why enduring love is so very difficult to obtain and maintain because most love affairs end in tears, and not marriage, with 50% of all marriages ending in divorce, with devastating consequences for children.

In addition to these terrifying statistics, very many couples who have managed to maintain an enduring relationship into old age, find it progressively more difficult to live in harmony. This is perhaps due to a growing fear of death, and dependence on others, whilst becoming infirm or immobile in old age is perhaps the ultimate indignity, which can only be removed by love.

Chapter 3

GOOGLE GENERATION

"There is faith, hope, and love, but the greatest is love." (Corinthians I, 13:13).

As Plato advises us, love is a serious disease, and it would be easy to come to the view that, because enduring love is extremely rare and requires patience, it is not possible for the Google generation, who appear to require Artificial Intelligence to acquire instant love and immediate gratification, while ignoring the emotional disequilibrium of social media or the hyper-immediate Cyberspace.

This misconception may be driven by the illusion of instant love being immediately available via online dating. This dangerous illusion is grasped as it rapidly passes through social media into believing the awful lie and philosophical heresy that one aspect of a physical loving experience is enough to build a sustainable relationship, within which you might perhaps one day fall in love and create children. This may be an exercise in wheel spinning without getting traction, because Agape or unconditional love, in addition to fusing together every dimension of love, is a meta-physical or a spiritual experience.

However, we must stand back a little because inactivity and not activity inspires wisdom, as the Bible tells us in Psalm 46 verse 10 "Be still and know," recommending a patient search for wisdom that may escape the hyper-activity of the Google generation.

The key point that this line from a great Psalm makes is that true knowledge is acquired by inactivity and not activity. Wisdom is an essential prerequisite for choosing happiness, but you will find that, as encapsulated in a statement attributed to Buddha:

"There is no path to happiness, because happiness itself is the path we must choose"

This challenge will question your strategy and your tactics, and whether it is a marriage, a career, or some other life changing decision you wish to make. I always ask myself the same question on my birthday, what do I want to be doing in three years' time? If the question has always been the same, then why are you wasting your time, spinning your wheels, just sitting and dreaming here?

Spiritual knowledge is born and grows from inactivity and not activity. The sad consequence is that the life-changing impact of understanding and enjoying all the many parts of love are seldom experienced due to a pursuit of instant gratification. After many years of counselling young people, I have come to the view that at a human level an enduring relationship is very difficult to create, and even more difficult to sustain. This very sad reality is validated by Scripture, with the awful warning we find in the Gospel of Matthew, 7:14.

"Straight is the gate and narrow is the way which leads to life, and few there be that find it"

Choosing happiness is the objective of this book, by examining the eight perspectives of love identified over thousands of years by ancient Greek philosophers and the Bible, which is also thousands of years old, some fearful and some beautiful. Do not search for the path to happiness, because happiness is the path. I trust this book will help a young person to seek an enduring unconditional love affair. It is vital that young people are briefed and made aware of the essential prerequisites of enduring love, before deciding to pursue a serious and or long-term relationship.

To understand an enduring relationship, we should recognize that life is dynamic and everything we see is moving, has moved, and will continue to move. These dynamic transitions must be carefully managed in a loving partnership because partners individually change, and the world around them changes, every hour of every day.

A major crisis time for a changing marriage is mid-life (45 - 55 years of age), when the children leave home, and the mother has time on her hands, while her husband's career may be under pressure from Artificial Intelligence, and more highly educated and more able young men. At this point, his dreams of greatness are overtaken by the horrors of reality, and all the lovers have left is the value they still recognize in each other, providing that a little love has survived during a progressive slow neglect of love in their relationship.
For two thousand years, the essence of Christian scholarship has been, *"God is love"* and we will be comparing this theological thesis with the eight secular Grecian perspectives of love. The ancient Greeks, led by Alexander the Great, having conquered most of the known world, turned to scholarship, and produced some of the greatest wisdom and philosophical concepts, the world has ever known.

The incisive nature of the results of their consolidated studies created a structure for their philosophy, leaving little to chance. In their religion, they created many Gods to love, made of marble, one for every challenge of love in the human condition, including one to *"The unknown God"* just in case they had missed one, and it angered the forgotten God. St. Paul addressed the futility of Polytheism, or worshipping many Gods, when debating with philosophers on Mars hill in Athens. Preaching the Christian Gospel, Paul said In AD 56 which is recorded in the, Acts of the Apostles:

"He who you ignorantly worship, I now declare unto you" (Acts 17:23)

Whilst the ancient Greeks developed their intellectual and imaginative resources to analyze what they believed were solutions to every human problem, these efforts failed when trying to understand the massive human complexity of love. The reason for their failure, is that love is not an intellectual challenge, and it defies intellectual analysis. It is a spiritual battle ground of the heart which mysteriously defies logic because it is the super-glue which joins and binds together every perspective and experience of our intellect and heart, as the following great man thought:

"The madness of love is the greatest of heaven's blessing" (Plato)

The piece of the jigsaw puzzle the Greek philosophers were unable to build into their model was the essential spiritual dimension of love, because it is not a unilateral experience, it is bilateral because love can only grow when united. We learn from Christian theology that we should love our neighbor, never forgetting that everyone qualifies as our neighbor, but God is love, which He shares with us, and we return by loving Him. When we involve another person, we create a trilateral constant flow and contra-flow of love, between us, God, and our neighbor, which energy drives evangelicalism.

This is a very great mystery and very difficult to understand because when the eight aspects of love identified by the Greeks merge together spiritually in our hearts, they embrace the fundamental principles of Christian theology. It was Aristotle who, while explaining the physics and mysteries of accelerated growth symbiotically uniting human hearts, revealed a very great secret of life.

"The whole is greater than the sum of the parts"

Jesus made a very similar statement indicating that the energy of a group was much greater than the sum of the like-minded people in the group. We were designed for community and fellowship, never meant to be alone, because when we live alone, we become smaller. Love expands our experience as Jesus made clear, that, while we may be physically alone, we are never alone or spiritually separated from the love of God.

"Where two or three are gathered in my name I am in the midst" (Matthew 18:20)

I recall from my time as a soldier in the British Army, the smallest unit of men is a squad which generally has a dozen soldiers because, after many thousands of years of killing each other, military commanders decided that twelve men living together became a family of very close brothers, and generated considerable additional energy with lasting deep, irreversible care for each other. The consequence is that a wounded man is never left to die alone on a battlefield, and many other close comrades are prepared to die trying to rescue him, and this is why veterans cry on remembrance days.

It is symbiosis, the secret of expanding love, when people deeply bond, and a flow and contra-flow of benevolent spiritual energy flows and grows exponentially between them. Symbiosis is an amazing experience and perhaps should be the targeted essence of every religious service.

Therefore, perhaps we might examine the intellectual analysis of the ancient Greek philosophers on the mysteries of love and compare their secular views with the spiritual insight of one of the greatest Biblical scholars who ever lived, the Apostle Paul, because he wrote more about love than any other man in history.

If you are not familiar with the Bible, I would like to respectfully introduce you to this great man Paul, because Christian theology provides the superglue which extracts the value and binds together the profound philosophy of the ancient Greeks.

Chapter 4

APOSTLE PAUL

"You have not chosen me, I have chosen you" (John 15:16)

It is the unique spiritual perspective of Paul that reveals love as a spiritual or meta-physical force of benevolent subtle energy, flowing and contra flowing between open benevolent hearts. Paul was an outstanding scholar and the beneficiary of four thousand years of highly detailed and carefully documented Jewish history and theology. He studied law at the University of Gamaliel in Jerusalem, and was fluent in several languages, Hebrew, Latin, and Greek.

After the crucifixion of Jesus, Paul became a temple policeman, violently opposing the young Christian church by torturing and killing Christian prisoners, who he considered were heretics, and to which murders he proudly confessed, by making this dreadful statement.

"I persecuted unto death both men and women" (Acts 22:4)

Paul was also present and participated in the murder of Stephen, the first victim of a generation of Christian martyrs. Paul's energy in persecuting Jewish Christians, was fueled by his hatred of any Jew who broke the law of Moses by abandoning rituals like circumcision, which is the essence of Jewish law, and God's covenant with Abraham. (Genesis 17:13). Paul was proud and passionate in what he believed was his murderous calling until, driven by hatred he had a near-death experience south of the ancient city of Damascus in Syria, after which his life was utterly transformed.

However, after coming to understand "Agape," grace or unconditional love, Paul faced a theological dichotomy, because as a Jew he was taught to believe that revenge was justified and that an "eye for an eye" was a proper and righteous judgment. (Exodus 21:24).

"A new commandment I give to you, that you love one another" (John 13: 34)

However, Agape, the love or grace of God, forgives transgressions unconditionally, and demands we turn the other cheek, forgiving and forgetting the pain and damage caused to us by others, without anger or retribution (Matthew 5:38-39). This contradicted the law of the Old Testament, which demanded retribution, until Paul introduced the concept of Grace to the world in the New Testament, which became so all-encompassing that it transcended every relationship, including the law, where the ritualism of Judaism was abandoned by Christians.

Two thousand years later, Mahatma Gandhi wisely said:

"If we follow an 'eye for an eye' philosophy, eventually the world would be blind"

This wisdom rapidly established a cornerstone of Christian theology, and Paul began to teach that we must learn to turn the other cheek and love our enemies, letting our painful memories go. Loving and forgiving became fundamental Christian principles, not designed for the benefit of our enemies, but our personal benefit. They are a model, teaching us to let accumulated disappointment go before the bitterness hurts us and begins to distort everything we value. Forgiving is not for the benefit of our enemies; it is for our benefit.

In the first century A.D. Paul introduced a monotheistic Judeo-Christian culture of love and forgiveness to Europe, which valued human life. Due to the power of love in the Christian Gospel the Christian Church spread exponentially and Europe became the great cradle of democracy and civilization. Paul provided the seeds of an alternative, God-centered, monotheistic belief for European culture opposed to cruelty, the low value of human life, and the Godless philosophical humanism of the Greco-Roman Culture.

In the Bible, the first letter Paul wrote to the Church in Corinth circa AD 54 provides profound insight into his character and the phenomena of the hidden mysteries of love, which Paul so dramatically experienced. Here is a brief extract from this letter, which is one of the most valuable observations on love we will ever be privileged to read:

> *"'Though I speak with the tongues of men and of Angels, and have not love, I am become as sounding brass, or tinkling symbol, and although I have the gift of prophecy, and understand all mysteries and all knowledge and though I have all faith, so that I could move mountains, and have not love - I AM NOTHING!"*
> *(1 Corinthians 13)*

We often forget that we are transparent and cannot hide or disguise who we really are. We are in plain sight, easily discovered by our opinions, reactions, the timbre of our voice and the neurolinguistics of our body language. We cannot hide our true feelings and identity by our focus or indifference to love in every word we use, or posture we adopt. We foolishly attempt to disguise who we really are by adopting a variety of masks, or personas we secretly carry around, often choosing, because of fear, who we would like to pretend to be today; I recall the wisdom of Nelson Mandela, when discussing fear:

> *"Courage is not the absence of fear, but the triumph over it"*

We will address the poetry and insight of Paul later in this book, but before we do, perhaps we might look at a couple of English romantic poets, because poets, philosophers, and theologians all speak in graphic pictorial metaphors from the non-physical, spiritual battlefield of their own hearts, and seldom write clearly describing the subject of their interest.

> *"In every person there is sunlight, just let it shine" (Plato)*
> *"How I do love thee, let me count the ways, I love thee to the depth and breadth of height, my soul can reach" (Elizabeth Barrett Browning)*

When trying to capture the essence of the soul, poets experience a subtle, metaphysical energy, of a flow and contra-flow, conveying and connecting extreme kindness and benevolence from comparable frequencies between one hungry heart to another.

As I have already mentioned, Love often originates as a logical first response to a perception of value when we see quality in another person, we would most like to possess ourselves because as Plato reminds us:

"We all have value"

As the Apostle John tells us, we can only learn of love by being loved:

"We love God because he first loved us" (1 John 4:19)

Failing to see and appreciate value in someone is illogical and may indicate that we are out of balance ourselves. Loving has a stabilizing effect on our emotions, but do we understand what it means to love, to be loved, or to be in love? The essence of Christian love is the awareness of the extent to which we have been loved by God, because of the value God saw in us. He created how we could fall in love with Him and because God's love is unconditional, it transcends all human experience of love, which is usually conditional.

We do not fall in love with people, but with the value we see in people, which are often perhaps some values we would like most to acquire for ourselves. However attractive attributes may appear, they often hide or disguise unattractive aspects, where love is blinded or distorted by Eros, or experience.

After this first encounter, we search for other attributes, which we may also love and wish to acquire, and our love towards that person develops and accelerates. If love is reciprocated, there is a flow and contra flow of energy, and we begin to fall in love because we now have so much to share and upon which we can build.

I am always puzzled when I see someone who is recovering from a bad relationship, choosing a partner with similar emotional problems to their previous partner. This appetite for pain is like the madness of putting two stones together and expecting them to float, or as we are reminded by the great Albert Einstein:

"Insanity is to do what we have always done but expecting a different result"

How can we possibly begin to understand a word like love which appears to mean and support so much, and yet means and supports so little? Life is dynamic and everything we see every day is moving, sadly relegating love to brief moments. Love requires space, patience, stillness, and knowledge by investing quality time to continually assure and be reminded that we are in love, because the biggest failure in maintaining enduring love, is neglecting to love.

However, because love, in any language, is a word most often misunderstood and misused, perhaps the best place for us to start our enquiry, is with the thoughts on love, debated and bequeathed to us by the greatest minds our world has ever known, who devoted their lives to thinking and debate.

There were many hundreds of philosophers, who lived peacefully during the golden years of the Greek Empire over two thousand years ago progressively acquiring ever greater wisdom over many centuries, by standing on the shoulders of their teachers.

These devoted scholars dedicated their lives over a period of five hundred years to exploring the intellectual, emotional, and physical mysteries of love in human relationships. The conclusion was that love could not be defined by one single word but needed a different word for every aspect of a loving experience or relationship.

Having only one word to express our feelings must mean it is impossible to express our feelings. We may love our dog, our spouse, our child, our mother, our job, our God, or even our neighbor, and we will embrace and encourage a totally different range of emotional experiences. If we say to someone dear to us, *"I love you,"* what exactly do we mean?

If we fail to understand that we only have one word to describe the greatest human experience, how can we possibly enjoy the many other dimensions of love, of which there are many, and we are ignorant? It is not a simple question of philosophy, or theology, it is a question of logic.

Every one of the eight aspect of love need to be comprehended and apprehended, before being symbiotically fused together, and absorbed into the essence of who we really are before materially enhancing our value, and the value of our relationships.

The incomprehensible paradox and mysterious secret of love is that it is not the beneficiaries of love who have the greatest experience of this secret joy, it is the benefactor. Paul said when meeting the elders of the church in Ephesus, to whom he declared his love for the last time before his death:

It is better to give than to receive" (Acts 20:35)

This is one of the great discoveries of the human condition, because in accepting this important principle we may feel a sense of obligation when accepting a gift, and generous when we give one. As Socrates said, we are afraid to love, and we build walls around us:

"Not to keep people in, but to see who cares enough to break them down"

A selfish person may find love, but never hold on to it because if love is not reckless it is not love, it is a relationship. If we are not prepared to recklessly put everything on the scales to discover what love really is, we are not ready for the experience.

The incredible joy of being loved will pass, because if love is ignored or rejected, it will never grow, it will quietly die, as we saw when we considered Shakespeare's words in Sonnet 116,

"Love is not love that alters when it alteration finds"

The bigger obstacle we hit is that Love must unite to expand. It is a one + one = one, bilateral equation, because it must embrace two essential elements with shared frequencies, and a common ambition to enlarge the life of each other.

During my time serving in the military, I had a friend who was a Christian. He told me that personal, self-interested prayers seldom change the heart and mind of God, but prayer always changes the heart and mind of the person who prays, because of the flow of grace the supplicant induces.

He prays every morning to renew and maintain his love of God and enjoys the bilateral experience of God's love to him throughout the day, which is a flow and contra-flow of grace and divine energy. It is, for him, love on wheels, as energy through comparable frequencies flows from him to God, but when he reads scripture the energy of God flows back to him, and I quote him here:

"It is where the rubber hits the road for me, and I am never the same again"

I have asked myself many times, how does the cornerstone of Christian theology, "God is love" impact upon my life? The answer I get is not always the answer I would like. If I truly took the time and believed that God influenced my life, I would love everyone I meet and everything I do, because there is value in everything I do, and everyone I meet, if I could just see it, but I certainly have a long way to go.

The single most important principle to remember, as we bring these thoughts to a close is fellowship, by which I mean a synthesis of bilateral energy when two strong forces meet and create a third larger entity of energy.

We see this in a marital union where physical symbiosis creates the third entity, namely a child, as Byron hints in his lovely poetry, validating that love must be a bilateral experience,

"Happiness was born a twin"

Byron reveals we can love while in isolation, but not be in love in isolation, because being in love requires another entity and is a boomerang which returns with stronger energy, reminding us that the only love we keep is the love we give way. Hate breeds hate, love breeds love, anger breeds anger, and the phenomenon of the creation of additional energy by symbiosis or union is most obvious with anger, when triggered by even the smallest event.

We were a large family, and my mother took in washing for two other families in our street, without a washing machine or dryer.

I would be fighting. My mother would tolerate this for a time, but occasionally, after her washing line broke and her clean clothes fell to the muddy garden and required re-washing she would come unglued.

This event would release all the accumulated disguised and hidden sadness of her life, and we would cease fighting for several days, because her anger was seldom experienced, but always best avoided.

For lovers of science, this is most clearly reflected in the third law of motion, expressed in the physics and theology of the great 17th century scientist Isaac Newton. He may have discovered the science of love when identifying the immense energy generated when love unites, as Newton's third law of motion states:

"Two objects interacting, exert equal and opposite forces on each other"

This means hate will always breed more hate, anger will always breed more anger, and lovers will always grow, surrendering and uniting in each other's arms enjoying the spiritual energy which accelerates exponentially as it expands.

A secret but important part of love is that if it does not unite, it cannot expand and cannot be shared with others, but more importantly we miss the immense value of experiencing the beauty of growing enduring love, Pragma, which we will deal with later in our book.

We may see or perhaps feel that we have experienced some aspects of the eight words for love offered by Greek philosophers to describe loving, or being loved, but we may also confess to some ignorance of being "in love" as an experience we have yet to experience, but let's try.

Chapter 5

EROS, SEX AND PHYSICAL ATTRACTION, OEDIPUS COMPLEX

Defraud not one another, that you are not tempted, (1 Corinthians 7:5)

Due to my own challenging experience as a teenager, I confess to having the greatest difficulty in considering a sexual experience as an act of love, for two basic reasons, science, and theology. The first is the scientific view of Sigmund Freud the Austrian neurologist, and father of psychoanalysis. Freud believed that human life ran on tension and pleasure, and for Freud it had nothing to do with an act of love or making love, because love cannot be made. He defined this tension as a product of sexual libido, or energy being built up within the body. His solution to this tension was a sexual release, or discharge of this energy.

The second is theological because in thousands of years of Judaic-Christian carefully documented history which deals with Spiritual love in an unequalled manner, sex is related to procreation or exploitation, but never to love.

We are trying to understand the eight vital aspects of love identified by the philosophy and the consolidated wisdom of the finest minds in our history. This task is being illuminated by thousands of years of Judaic-Christian theology and history, but we need to confront Eros with the crime of high-jacking the illusion of love and abandoning it for sexual appetites, which are unsustainable.

Eros is the Greek word from which we get our word Erotic which fuels a drive for sex and has nothing to do with love. Eros, or erotic, are used extensively in the Greek and English language for physical relationships, but seldom for love.

The challenge we have in describing Eros as love in a physical union, makes it impossible for us to describe a sexual experience as making love, because it has to do with lust and nothing to do with making love, it is illogical nonsense.

If love could be made it would be much more than a sole isolated transient physical experience, disappointing when one partner is misused or undervalued, reducing the perceived worth of a participant. If making love was possible it would be a flow and contra-flow of benevolent Spiritual, and emotional energy with the sole objective of enhancing the life and value of the person with whom we are sharing our body and our life.

Since the beginning of time, sex has been a currency and tradable commodity and sustainable industry in every culture on earth, and therefore prostitution is the oldest profession, of which love has never claimed to be a part. It is important to note of the eight parts of our analysis of love, Eros is a very small part of the total experience, upon which the Greeks choose to focus, and Christians and Jews choose to ignore.

Making love in five minutes, or five hours, is impossible because a spiritual experience cannot be mechanically or intellectually assembled. The only way to make love is to assemble our history and destiny together, punctuated with Biblical texts and the building blocks chosen by the Greek philosophers in our diagram and bind them together with someone who means more to us than life itself.

I cannot write of my own first experience of sex or so-called physical love. It was dreadful, because I was emotionally and psychologically violated, at a young and impressionable age and from which I have never fully recovered or spoken of, until today.

It was just after the war in Europe, I was an eighteen-year-old soldier serving as a Military Police Officer with British special forces in the largest Adriatic Sea port of the City of Trieste, in Northern Italy. The British army were occupying and defending the city, which was rioting, encouraged by the Communist party in Italy and the Communist Yugoslavian army, camped at the border, and who were planning to invade northern Italy, but thankfully they didn't.

Notwithstanding, the warships we had in the port, we only had the military resources to hold the city for forty-eight hours. However, the primary logistical challenge was not an invasion, but the exponential spread of venereal disease among young British and American soldiers and sailors. which meant too many servicemen were becoming ill, reporting unfit for service, with many new infections being reported every day. Apparently, this was a phenomenon which occurred with victorious occupying armies after every war.

Soldiers were allowed out of barracks, and sailors from British warships at 5:00 pm for six hours every day and there were always large groups of teenaged girls at the gates, anxious to meet young soldiers and sailors, and Italian teenage girls can be very attractive to such young men. While there were older prostitutes amongst them, most of the younger girls were not selling sex, but looking for marriage.

These naive young British military personnel were responsible for spreading most of the infections, because for several weeks after they contacted the disease, one serviceman, unaware he was infected, could often infect several other girls on a weekly basis; the girls would then go on to infect other British service men, moving to new partners.

As the problem was spreading exponentially, an anti-vice squad was formed uniting the American and British Military Police who were given the responsibility, with exceptional legal powers, to halt the spread of the disease. This required infected sick soldiers and sailors to report where they had met the infected girls, and the girls they had subsequently infected, but it would often take a month for the symptoms of the disease to manifest. The Military Police had to locate and arrest the girls and the servicemen, who would remain in custody until after they recovered from the medication provided by the British Military Hospital. Brothels were legal in Italy, and brothels were out of bounds to British and American service men.

However, this military restriction was largely ignored by military personnel because there were far too many houses of ill repute for the Military Police Vice Squad to monitor, and they were opening more rapidly than they we could close them. When an infection was located, we would raid the brothel and arrest the girls and any British or U.S. serviceman in the building. This often resulted in fierce hand to hand fighting, and offers of bribes, which I am pleased to say were never taken, although they would have subsidized the very small wages, we were being paid by the army.

As with other teenaged soldiers I had never had a girlfriend, having left my mother just a few months earlier for the first time, and I was now involved in raiding brothels, getting physically hurt, and hurting others, in pitched battles with prostitutes, and bouncers, many of the latter ex-professional boxers. They were supported by wealthy brothel owners who were fighting to avoid arrest and being prevented from pursuing their profession.

The older women were largely war widows, who fought more viciously against arrest than any man I had encountered in my military service, often removing all their clothes because naked they knew the policemen would not touch them, because of the fear of cross infection, and allegation of sexual assault. However, the military was always able to succeed by throwing more men at the problem, and the ladies were eventually hand-cuffed, before being wrapped in army blankets and formally arrested by armed teenaged boys, wearing military uniforms.

Notwithstanding the fact that we threw ourselves intellectually and emotionally at the challenge and successfully began to slow the rate of infections, we ignored the psychological effect upon ourselves. I ceased writing a weekly letter to my mother, because I was aware, she would know that something was wrong, as I always wrote to her explaining the work in which I was involved, which I ceased to do. I began to avoid interviewing or interrogating women, because I could not look into their eyes. I hated interrogating prostitutes because they became violent, always lied, and often carried weapons, but although they knew when they were infected, they deliberately and knowingly continued to infect young sailors and soldiers, which made me intensely angry and created a level of violence in me I did not understand, and often failed to control.

My primary recollection of those dark days were the confused hopes and aspirations of teenaged boys regarding the incomprehensible mysteries of young women, who were having sex, and infecting young British service men, participating in an illusion of love. This confusion of what is love, was certainly influenced by the first love I had for my mother who for many years was the only love I experienced.

The Oedipus Complex
This unproven, Greek/Egyptian thesis has been around for thousands of years, and allegedly becomes evident when a child develops a strong attachment to a parent of the opposite sex, identified by envious and aggressive feeling towards a parent of the same sex.

This tension created a cloud which eliminated my ambitions and provided no access to my future, which had been stolen by my progressive hatred of women, to whom sex appeared to be a currency. It was also in direct conflict with the close relationship I had with my mother. I punished myself every day because perhaps I had crossed the line and loved my mother too much and loved my father too little. However, for ten years after the death of my mother, I would visit her grave on her birthday and leave poems I had written to her, which I had hidden in the flowers I had bought at the gates of the cemetery, the following is just one of many:

Birthday
This day is no exception.
It began far too early,
And will continue, far too long.
Painfully the same,
As other anniversaries.
I am drifting motionless,
In a wretched vacuous void,
Haunted by the tearful news,
the sunlight of my life has gone,
bequeathing mocking memories.
There is a fracture in the marrow of my bones
an alien force is sipping all my blood,
My heart crushed when you slipped away
My life force, draining to the ground,
as I call and reach for you.

One day, I was given "Mourning and Melancholia," by Sigmund Freud, after which I went to my mother's grave and said, "thank you, but I love you enough to set you free." However, I was sure that sex must never be confused with love because they are at the absolute opposite ends of the spectrum of love and life.

Had it not been for the influence of the godly sixteen-year-old girl to whom I will refer at the end of this book, who after four years of sitting by me in church, slowly put me back together, and became my wife, I would never have recovered the deep respect I have always had for women, and allowed that awful period of my life, still all too vivid in my memory, and often disturbing my sleep, to slip into the shadows.

Like most ex-service men, I was demobilized from the Army with PTSD, feeling far too emotionally contaminated and afraid to explain to my mother my challenges in Italy. While she knew something was wrong, I was unable to share with her my anger, or be helped by her, and I recalled an old Italian proverb, which advice I failed to adopt.

"If you are bleeding, find a man with scars"

Unless our relationships begin as teenagers when we are maturing slowly and beginning to adjust in a relationship with one mind, we always carry some baggage and emotional damage from our own childhood, parents or previous relationships. This may require some healing and loving care and if this is so we must make sure that our partner is a carer and has adequate emotional reserves, to share our healing process.

The question is, are we building this relationship together, or is what we have enjoyed together slowly slipping away? if you listen, the answer to the question will speak loudly from your heart. The heart never lies, but we always suffer when we lie to ourselves, because self-deception is the worst kind of dishonesty. There are questions we perhaps should address such as, are we progressing in our relationship, or retreating, and if it is slipping away from us, do we have the time and the will to put it right?

The challenge with residual bitterness is, when it is tucked away in our subconscious, it can, in times of pressure, allow a lifetime of anger and bitterness to be downloaded in a few minutes. The best advice is to listen with our hearts, but we must have the courage to share with our partner how we feel and agree in love what needs to happen to grow our love and to ensure it is sustainable.

Eros signifies physical union, believed by ancient Greeks to describe only one aspect of the experience of loving, being loved, and being in love. It was not self-interest or gratification which attracted the philosophical scholars, it was simply the pursuit of beauty and truth which attracted them. The challenge we have is that the Eros experience of love can be easily highjacked and illusory, with the consequence being that many of the children born from an unholy counterfeit of love can spend a great deal of time as adults looking for love they will seldom find. Love can never be recognized if it has never been seen or experienced in action and reciprocated, in a flow and contra-flow of meta-physical energy.

If a child is not conceived in love, but by accident, or irresponsibility, the residual scars left behind by the separation and neglect of parents will insulate the child from learning to love or trusting their own emotions. If the Eros experience is not comprehensive and equally shared it may only be a single and extremely limited perspective and experience of one dimension of love, sustained by an appetite for the illusion of physical pleasure.

This may satisfy short term self-interest, by providing a transient illusion of love. Potentially it may carry very high emotional costs because the flower of love cannot grow and multiply in soil fertilized by the suffering and pain of others, leaving a child born out of wedlock potentially without adequate parental care or love. I am always surprised by the selfish naivety of people who walk away from a marriage or relationship and their children, which separation creates continuous suffering for those who remain, while they try to find a happy life in a new family, having just destroyed an old one. One of the greatest emotional and illogical mysteries people adopt is to believe happiness can be built on the suffering of a child, or a partner whose life they have so badly, and perhaps irreversibly damaged.

The great danger in this kind of liaison is that it may be transient because a single illusion of physical love is not sustainable without the spiritual super-glue to bind all the many parts of a relationship together and fuel its growth. Real, or comprehensive love is dynamic and must be constantly maintained and continually developed, juxtaposed to an unfulfilled transient physical liaison not being fueled and thus getting smaller, until it disappears completely.

This has dreadful consequences where children are involved, because they pick up the bill for the tragedy of a mid-life, and miserable, self-interested generation. It is inconceivable just how carelessly some parents treat a commitment to a child, which should be a life-long, continually growing and beautiful relationship, trading it instead for short term pleasure at the expense of the children involved. Love cannot be taught because it is the natural synthesis of our intellectual and emotional resources. The reason Eros love must involve the additional super-glue of spiritual love to be sustainable is because it is often demonstrated in front of children. Love, like anger or hatred, can only be learned by observation, or by direct involvement.

In the United Kingdom and the United States, approximately half of the people cohabiting and producing children are unmarried, and half of the people who are married and producing children will separate or divorce. This cruel drama is being powerfully accelerated by a change in UK divorce and civil contracts laws, where marriage can now be cancelled much more easily than cancelling an unwanted hire purchase agreement. Last year in the United Kingdom for the first time in history more people divorced than were married. This breakdown in parental relationships will have long term immeasurable and devastating consequences for the children losing one parent, who stand as innocent bystanders of an unholy union, which at some past time masqueraded as love.

This experience irreplaceably steals from a child the opportunity of ever discovering love because love must be recognized and experienced to be understood. The very last part of a breakdown in a relationship between conflicting partners is the consequence of the tragedy of disappearing love upon the psyche of their children. There can be fewer more serious crimes than destroying the hopes and aspirations of a child.

Innocence is torn from terrified child bystanders as they watch their only experience of love suddenly turn to verbal violence and hatred, or perhaps sometimes turns to nothing, but a dark vacuum of fear and loneliness. Children cannot understand why the absolute certainty of the permanence of love dramatically evaporates before their eyes, and in consequence have no wish to witness, or ever trust the illusion of love again.

There is one more sad experience of counterfeited evaporating love which a child may have to endure, which is being forced to be an unwilling partner of conflicting parents to fill the role of "love football". This is the mistaken belief that hurting the child is the most effective way of hurting the other parent.

A damaging by-product of the game is the child will learn the rules of love football and inevitably learn to manipulate and eventually control the conflicting parents. However, the child will always be plagued by the curse of manipulation imposed by selfish parents on their young hearts and minds.

I had a medical friend who was a highly regarded expert in ante-natal matters, and he told me that an unborn child experiences everything the pregnant mother feels. If she takes drugs or smokes, or drinks alcohol so does the unborn infant, and the logic was simple to accept. What was not so simple to accept was that the consequence of the expectant mother being emotionally stressed is that it can also disturb the peace and security of her unborn child. If this is so, a simple unkind look from a father to be may have a negative impact upon the child, but why take the risk, love your expectant spouse unconditionally, and accept the immense privilege of bringing a child into a family of love. as Paul says in his letter to the Christian church in Rome:

"Be kindly affectionate one to another" (Romans 12:10)

Sadly, although conflicting partners may win or lose regular battles, they will both lose the war, because the war will be lost in the irreparable damage their self-interest has upon children of the union, who will be scarred for life. The scars are manifested in many ways, but by far the most common is that children blame themselves when love disappears from a family, believing that if they had been better behaved, the absent parent would still be at home. If a child in its formative years feels the loss of love, there is no refuge to be found for the essential security a child must feel to avoid laying a foundation of low self-esteem. Low self-worth will never leave a child and may affect every judgment the child will ever make, because they will always feel unworthy of a task given to them.

The evidence of this psychological trauma may not become evident until teenage years when, due to low self-worth, the child searching for love will think they are less attractive than they are. They may imagine another persona, often telling lies or distorting reality for their emotional comfort.

I have known many cases where teenaged children of professionally driven parents have felt emotionally deprived and betrayed and in consequence gone off to find love. In many of these cases the girls found only sex and children of their own, and the boys joined the army, or a police force, to find an illusion of brotherhood. Almost all children feel a sense of responsibility and guilt when a parent leaves home or neglects them and, due to a perception of low self-worth, many self-harm or even end their lives. I had two close friends, highly educated and successful men who, after their marriages failed, lost teenage daughters who committed suicide. One of them, a medical doctor who spent his life healing others, said that he and his wife waited until the children were in bed before discussing their marital problems, only to discover their teenaged daughter had been sitting on the stairs for months listening to her parents fight.

One grey December day she could bear it no more and killed herself; some months later my friend made one of the shortest, saddest comments I have ever heard, when he said, "I wish I had my time again."

Another old friend, an outstanding scholar who became a very successful minister of a church had a highly intelligent son and two lovely teenaged daughters. one of whom surprised him one day by saying, *"We make a date with your secretary, to get a meeting with our own Dad."* When I challenged my friend, he betrayed a defect in his thinking, by saying, *"If I do God's work, in Gods way, God will take care of my family."*

Sadly, this failed to happen, because it is parents and not God who are responsible for loving and guiding the lives of the children we choose to bring into the world. My friend was too close to the challenge to see the defect in his thinking, and I reminded him of the first letter Paul wrote to his protégé, the young man Timothy, when Paul said:

"He who cares not for his own family is worse than an unbeliever" (1 Timothy 5:8)

My friend's children left home in their search for love and the girls became pregnant by men who chose to abandon the responsibilities they had created. His son joined the army, and later the police force in search of a caring family, which he failed to find. He divorced his wife, who committed suicide, and his children separated, during which time he retreated into alcohol, perhaps to hide from the reality of his difficult legacy, and the misery of his isolation in the family he had created.

I have often wondered how a human life should be examined. Should it be for good works, or the quality of life achieved by children because they have been intellectually, and spiritually prepared for the challenge of love and life?

"An unexamined life is not worth living" Socrates

Paul makes it clear in his letter to the Ephesians:

"Provoke not your children to wrath but bring them up in the nurture and admonition of the Lord" (Ephesians 6:4)

Before he died my friend, who was the author of some twenty books, shared with me his despair for failing to understand the responsibility he had for his children, juxtaposed to his calling to write and teach as an academic and a church leader. This is a very sad story for me, and it still hurts, because I could have done more to help him, but only by experience and honest observation is education and wisdom available to us.

Understanding love is the heart and essence of education, and although self-interest may come from the most noble ideals and relationships, it may still be a matter of self-interest.

Sadly, towards the end of his life there was little time to unite and grow the love I know he had for his children, or their love for him, because love is both powerful and dynamic and if it fails to unite and expand, it cannot sustain itself.

It is children who pay the price for neglected love, but the pain does not end with them. Regrettably, in due course it may be adopted by their own children because the vacuum of love created by indifference is often passed to grandchildren from generation to generation, painfully growing in the process.

At some time in our lives, we are all likely to contribute to the life of a child, but we perhaps fail to realize the impact of our influence upon the child, who will adopt our balance or imbalance of love because being loved is the only interest of a child. We cannot hide or disguise who we are, and a sensitive child will absorb the influence of parental trauma by paradoxically adopting the disequilibrium we so irresponsibly create, and bequeath, to our children.

The most important message I trust we have shared, is that love breeds love, and self-interest breeds self-interest, and we cannot successfully masquerade as someone else by putting on a mask, because the new persona, without any substance, will sound hollow because it is hollow, and will eventually implode.

We inevitably impose our values, or our pain, on our children, after which these challenges are repacked and passed to our grandchildren, with compound interest. Beware therefore, that what goes around comes around. if you plant daffodils don't expect tulips to flower. It is a profound philosophical principle of the ancient Greek thinkers, also the Karma of Buddhism, and theology of Christianity, that the day will come from which no one will ever escapes. We reap what we sow.

Chapter 6
PHILIA (AFFECTION)

"Parents do not provoke or discourage your children" (Colossians 3:21)

"Expect no positive response, the reward for loving is love itself" (Anon)

"Above all things have charity among yourselves" (1 Peter 4:8)

When we use the term "love" for an inanimate object such as, I love my job, my new car, or my home, Philia (affection) is the word the Ancient Greeks would have used. Although there might be a strong flow of loving beneficence to the object of that love, there is no contra-flow, we get nothing in return, because it is not bilateral, it is a unilateral experience, a one-way street, with love flowing only in one direction.

This is only half of the story because when we use the word love, in that I love my dog, my cat, my horse, my goldfish or my garden, we really mean affection. We are inclined to forget that for love to grow, it must be with a living entity, there must be a flow and contra-flow of benevolent energy, which calls for growth because love is dynamic and never stands still, it either precedes or recedes.

To illustrate my point, my wife and I have had two cats from tiny kittens, one adopted by my wife and one by me, thus creating two distinctly separate monogamous relationships. Cats, like humans have strong self-interests, which is the anti-thesis of love, but we have found this self-interest has progressively disappeared as the cats grow closer to a single loving owner. When I have discussed with my friends the love we have for our pets, I have been surprised by the love people have for their cats and dogs and even goldfish, and how long their grief and sense of loss continues after the death of a pet.

For many years we lived on a farm and to fully enjoy the countryside we bred horses, and our children had ponies, for which they accepted sole responsibility to feed, clean and care. The reason we strictly followed this plan was that a pony would never kick or bite a child who cared for it, because of the flow-and contra-flow of benevolent loving energy which passed between them. My wife was afraid of horses and telegraphed her fear subconsciously, and this flow and contra-flow of negative energy, caused them both to be afraid of each other.

Another example of the flow and contra-flow of energy is the secret life of plants, which theory unjustifiably created some amusement when HRH Prince Charles (as he then was) allegedly stated that he talked to his plants. In his defense, may I say, I have been privileged to visit his home in Gloucestershire, and I have never seen more beautiful wild-flower meadows, and so whatever mysteries Prince Charles had employed to create such beauty, harmony, and butterflies, they certainly appeared to be working.

Without green plants we would not be able to breathe because trees and leaves, in a miracle of photosynthesis, produce oxygen from absorbing carbon dioxide, giving us the life and food that we enjoy, and often take for granted.

In 350 BC Aristotle wrote a treatise on the soul, which he identified in plants and different kinds of living things, distinguished by their different operations.

In 1961, Simon Kirlian, a Russian engineer, published a patent on a camera that photographed energy fields around flowers. This aura changed in color, depending upon the health of the plant, which was affected by the water, and the care and attention it received. Curiously, if a leaf was cut in half, a new photograph continued to show the energy field of the whole leaf before amputation. This may mean that essential data could be retained in the Aura, or energy field and perhaps one day we may be able to photograph the soul and establish the true and early cause of illness.

Aristotle argued that the soul is never absent from its living host, because it is the creative form or essence of any living thing, including plant life. Aristotle believed that thinking and loving are our fundamental human responsibilities, because of the damage or joy we create when we impose our thoughts and life force on the targets and beneficiaries of our love. It is perhaps simultaneous thinking and loving which possessed the quintessentially romantic English poets to be affected by Aristotle's view of the soul of flowers or herbs, which unlike humans, when trampled upon, always respond with a loving fragrance.

> **"One is nearer to God in a garden than any other place on earth" Gurney**
>
> **"Roses are red violets are blue, honey is sweet so are you" Edward Spence**
>
> **"My heart with pleasure fills, and dances with the daffodils" Wordsworth**

Little was heard of the soul of flowers for two thousand years, until Charles Darwin (1800) proposed that plants and trees and every tendril of a plant had a power of independent movement, but only became active in their own self-interests, which are unseen, due to the slow pace of their movements. Flowers are undoubtably a metaphor and means of conveying what our hearts and the eloquence of our poetry wants to say when we cannot assemble the right words for ourselves, and we need to express an additional depth of our emotions. Flowers may be a symbol of our love in the hands of a bride, or when visiting the sick, or to carry our tears in mourning when some experience of love has passed from us.

I recall an ironic line from a humorous poem mourning the absence of love, validated by the absence of flowers:

> **"Look, the flowers you nearly bought, have lasted all this while" (Cope)**

Flowers are powerful eloquent metaphors, and Aristotle explained the mystery of metaphors which, although intellectually challenging, reveal to us exactly what they are:

"An act of genius, implying an intuitive perception of similarity in the dissimilar"

This reminds me that the way most of us learn to love is by being first loved, because from our earliest consciousness we experience the love and care of our parents, who were overwhelmed by the perceived value of their creation. Being the beneficiary of an immense flow of love a child cannot help but feel loved and of great value and is the most important of all educational experiences. A child with a perception of high self-esteem is a child who is confidently approaching the challenges of life, and we can only gain this confidence by being first loved. **(1 John 4:19).**

A child feels only gratitude for the food and comfort it first receives. However, the child quickly learns to be grateful, and the mother begins to feel the love of her child develop. Both the child and the parents begin to experience the flow and contra-low of subtle energy and are in a state of being in love. I suspect that all plants, trees and perhaps all living organisms share the same experience, advancing when cared for or retreating when neglected.

There is no doubt that positive and negative subtle energy exists; the American Indians put their backs on trees when exhausted, and curiously some women going into a house or garden for the first time will feel whether it has been a happy or unhappy home because for some people, the energy is eloquent. It is therefore not difficult to accept that a living tree or plant searching and growing up to reach the sun at the same time reaching down to find water, has some form of essence which reacts to being cared for, or ignored.

Perhaps the reason we may find this difficult to accept is because we do not understand how humans and plants respond to loving and being loved. Our failure to understand is perhaps because we have come to believe the opposite to love is to hate. However, this is a mistake, because love like hate involves passion, which having similar emotions feeds upon itself and increases in volume, because we are reluctant to let the strength of our emotions fade. We feel cheated long after love has gone, and we need to hang on to the remnants of our transient passion and experience of love.

Some years ago, I was on a long-haul aircraft for twelve hours sitting by a lady who was distressed with flying and insisted on telling me a story of the breakdown of her marriage and her husband's infidelity, and how much she hated him. She accused him of stealing her most important years and I attempted to console her by suggesting that time would heal, and if she chose happiness and not sadness, she could have a great life. I was surprised to learn her divorce had occurred five years previously, but clearly, from the passion she retained, she was still emotionally connected to her husband, or perhaps she loved the state of being "In love," and had no wish to move on.

However, the experience of being in love had long ago died, perhaps through neglect, but she could no longer carry the pain, clearly finding relief downloading her distress to a stranger, like me. I suggested she adopt the most important philosophical axiom ever agreed or proclaimed, which was to forgive her enemies, not for the sake of her enemies, but for her sake, otherwise it will make happiness impossible. She was swimming in an ocean chained to a dead man but life with him was over.

She cried and promised to love him and let him go, and I shared with her that happiness is a choice, because the world is a mirror, smile and the world will smile back.

The most profound line of any poem I have ever read was by John Donne who I mentioned earlier, but should be regularly repeated, because happiness is a choice:

"Be your own palace, or the world will be your jail"

This will enable us to see the world through different eyes and move on to find love again by seeing quality in others, without the baggage or the anger and bitterness of our history. Anger is the most awful and effective model to halt our growth to a full experience of love, and lasting happiness.

I am pleased to share with you one of the greatest secrets and mysteries of life which is that the opposite of love is not hate, the opposite to love is indifference. If we want a plant or a love affair to blossom and perfume our lives, we must feed it daily with our hands and our hearts, but if we want it to die, just ignore it, without anger, and mourn the passing, because it is the funeral of an old friend.

Chapter 7

STORGE AND FAMILY LOVE

"The family is the first cell of human society" Pope John XXIII

"Two cannot walk together unless they are agreed" (Amos 3:3)

"There is no doubt that it is around the family and the home, that all the greatest virtues are created, strengthened, and maintained" (Winston Churchill).

"Family love is the music of harmony" (Friedrich Nietzsche).

"The whole is greater than the sum of its parts" (Aristotle).

What Aristotle was saying was that love between two people feeds upon itself, but this accelerates when members of a loving family meet, due to the congruous frequencies they have built. This is also experienced in groups, like churches or golf clubs where members are united and bound by a common interest. What Aristotle identified and explained was a mystery in physics until it was discovered fifteen hundred years later, by Sir Isaac Newton, who said:

"When two objects interact, they exert equal and opposite forces on each other"

This profound discovery is never more clearly exposed than in a family because it is the consequence of a loving relationship between siblings where people in harmony create an additional strength and which gives a family more energy and unity than they individually might contribute in a family. Truly something for nothing, created by the love and unity of fellowship. The challenge with creating additional energy by unity, is what kind of energy are we choosing to create, because the choice is always in our own hands.

We choose to meet in love, hate, or indifference, often in family gatherings at Thanksgiving, Christmas or special events, which sometimes end in tears, because of self-interest or indifference, which are the anti-thesis of loving. It is because of the effect that "equal and opposite forces" have upon each other that we will clash and disagree, because in a family we have a similar genetic memory and DNA and we all resemble each other in some way or other, but we are all uniquely different. It is this unique difference, which requires great wisdom for parents to understand and negotiate by first identifying the differences and adjusting to them in enlarging the harmony and growth of energy in the family.

This requires great wisdom, because the first-born will always be aware they are the first-born and will always occupy a special place, competing with dad for mum's attention. This may validate the Oedipus complex of Sigmund Freud, who believed it may have a significant influence on the development, of a male first born child. Many young husbands may feel as I did, putting off having a child because of a fear that for a woman, love was a limited resource and that after the first child arrived, the love the husband enjoyed would be put on the back burner, never to be recovered.

However, this is a defective premise because, in my case the reverse applied. I recall one night, after putting our first newly born son on the pillow between us my wife saying to me, "when I look at him, I see only you, and when I look at you, I see only him".

Perhaps understandingly we went on to have four children, followed by many grandchildren, and great-grandchildren, with whom my wife and I have shared the experience of the love we have discovered together, and now see in them.

On that night I learned something very important about women and love, which is a woman's capacity for loving is as elastic as it is limitless, because no matter how many children she has, her emotional resources magically grow to allow her to love them all just the same, and never at the expense of her husband's fragile male psyche, or his fear of rejection in the love they share.

The other challenge parents have in lovingly building a family is that the intellectual resources and emotional reserves of siblings vary considerably. The first child will always be treated as a miracle of creation, with a power base the second child cannot adopt or avoid. This means the second child must make more noise just to get noticed and be heard, which the second child may consider to be a little unfair. This illusion and aggressive need for equality may create in a second child a rejection of parental authority, and a subsequent and dangerous rejection of all authority and an excessively competitive nature, affecting character and life.

Undoubtably by far the biggest challenge for a first-born child is having a successful father, who cannot help but cast a very long shadow over his child, who perceives he will never fill his father's shoes, and so he never tries. The biggest mistake that father's make is to believe that his son has no part of his mother in him and is intolerant of the evidence when it appears. If a mother is the wife of a high achiever, she has the very great task of protecting and making a high achiever of her child by encouraging and exposing every success the child may have, whether in mathematics, swimming, or football or any subject in which the child expresses interest, because the child will never stand in their father's shoes, but they may stand tall in their own.

Sadly, parents cannot be all things to all men, and they cannot disguise who they are and what they are thinking. In my case I am dyslexic, which my father thought was brain damage, at a time when my siblings won scholarships to higher education. My transparently honest father was unable to change the look of pride in his eyes when talking to my siblings, and the deep sadness in his eyes when talking to me.

However, Grace intervened early in my life, and the emotional detachment from my father drove me into my mother's extra-loving arms because it is always the disabled child who gets the extra love.

This was a delightful, life transforming experience born from my mother's continually recited mantra:

> *"You must never feel inferior, without your own consent"*

I went from a position of isolation and low self-esteem to a position of value I felt in my mother's arms which has never left me, because I would never have traded my experience of her love for the high academic accolades won by my siblings.

I ceased to be fearful of my father and most other matters because every day my mother told me I was cleverer than all my siblings and I eventually believed her because it was all I wanted to hear. After this, I acquired confidence, and an appetite for the adrenaline of risk, and a dangerous lack of fear of all authority, which has never left me. At eighteen I dreamed of having authority by joining the Army and I became a Military Policeman, and I was often surprised in very dangerous situations at the fear of my comrades, which I did not experience, but having no fear is dangerous because I was hurt on occasions when punching above my weight.

The most challenging time for children to be loved is during their teenaged years, when the desire for autonomy and power is strong, and the wisdom of parents is most vital but most often rejected. This is a time when children choose careers, and partners, on which their future happiness depends, often unacceptable to their loving or ambitious parents, but children must choose and learn to deal with losing for themselves.

I was reminded of this recently when I talked to one of my grandsons, who is thinking of a career in finance and had arranged to spend the summer as an intern with a large accounting and consulting firm. After this perhaps dull and boring six-month period, he will be either passionate for a career in finance, or he will reject it and examine many other related options available to ambitious young people like him. I recall in my military training my commanding officer saying:

> *"If you do not prepare to win, you are preparing to lose"*

One of the biggest challenges in parenting is raising an only child, because the child will become the sole beneficiary of the overwhelming love of two parents, and because it is very difficult to comparably respond, the child doesn't comparably respond, it is a one-way relationship with everything to lose, by love flowing only one way, and nothing more to gain.

Siblings are a very important part of the development of a child because to "belong," children must learn to contra-flow in love and compromise, by giving as much, or more than they take, and they very quickly learn. Not from parents but from peers, life is a competitive sport, and early privilege can be a serious disadvantage, and I am grateful I struggled so much, when I was young.

If a family is limited to only one child it is important that child attend nursery school as early as possible, to relate to other children of the same age, because to learn the fundamental principles of a happy life a child must be prepared to negotiate and adjust to the wishes of others.

Another error that a parent in a larger family makes is treating every child in the same way, which undoubtably, in fairness, would seem to be the most equitable and righteous thing a parent could do to. However, this is based on the defective premise that all children are the same, and that they should all be treated the same way.

A first child, being loved, may become a perfect child, but a second child living in the shadow of a sibling may fight to be heard, become competitive and difficult to love. A parent needs to find the wisdom to guide each sibling as a special need's child, recognizing and encouraging the unique intelligence and undeveloped amazing imagination of every individual child.

My wife and I made a dreadful mistake, with our twin sons who we not only treated in the same way, but we dressed them the same until, at twelve years of age, we realized our mistake and sent them, at their request, to different schools.

The first reaction to this move was their pleasure at being called by their individual names and not just referred to as one of the twins. There is no doubt that our failure as parents to treat our twin sons as separate individuals delayed identifying their natural gifts, and career choices, for some years. I am pleased to report that this early reversal proved to be a powerful driver because they have both been very successful in their career choices, one as a businessman, and the other a Barrister, and now a Judge.

A final word on the challenges of having only one child; love is not a one-way street and to receive all the love parents can provide, the child must do nothing but to sit back and enjoy the love and energy of others. However, the child must be taught that love is an enduring partnership, which grows, or recedes daily directly proportionate to the time that the partners invest in the relationship.

This is not the fault of an only child, but it makes enduring relationships very difficult to maintain, and marriage failures of only children are statistically high. However, due to inbred self-interest, a marriage between two only children, requires extraordinary generosity on the part of the partners, or it will die.

I spent some years of my career working in the USA, and I observed that, at parties, people often would "do the room," which means that they come up to you and ask three or four key questions, before moving on or remaining, assessing whether friendship with you may be of value to them, in their aggressive pursuit of self-interest.

However, as time passes, children begin to understand that love is not a self-centered one-way street requiring no contribution from anyone. Sadly, we all have experience of people who seldom expect to contribute to a friendship and only expect to benefit. Growing love requires a response because it is a flow and contraflow of subtle energy which must unite, with a comparable force, or it will never expand.

During my life I have counselled many people, most of whom were young teenagers, whose parents were high achieving personal friends in academia, politics, medicine, or business. In almost every case the young people were underperforming, and I discovered that it was not the children who were delinquent, it was the parents, who were far too busy in pursuing personal or professional objectives, to love and raise a child, notwithstanding they claimed it was all for the benefit of the family, which was breaking down.

An early career possibility exciting a teenager with a simple sensible strategy is validated by the wisdom of the great Chinese philosopher Confucius. It was two thousand five hundred years ago, who advised us we will always achieve success if we do what we love doing, when he said:

"If you love what you do, you will never have to go to work"

Chapter 8

MANIA AND OBSESSIVE LOVE

Pray without ceasing (1 Thessalonians 5:17)

Perfect love casts out all fear, there is no fear in love, (1 John 4:18)

"Let your dreams be led by reason." Cicero

Mania is the most difficult form of love to understand because it is intellectually incomprehensible, whilst being diagnostically an indication of emotional imbalance, and some level of mental illness, because it may create dangerous or irrational behavior.

Love has many vital parts, and Mania is a very important part to understand because it can transcend all reason, logic, and experience. It may also be an obsessive, highly dangerous and very powerful form of focus, creating imbalance and lack of control. We cannot influence what comes into our minds, which is the way the dictionary describes Mania:

"Ideas continually intruding into a person's mind"

There are all sorts of examples of obsessive love, which are usually based on pursuing some illusive objective we desire and may involve illegal behavior such as stalking another person, or passionately focusing on some specific opportunity. If we look more closely at Mania, we see obsession and focus as two dimensions of the word which are great attributes of love when applied to noble causes, but highly dangerous when applied to ignoble or unreasonable opportunities. I doubt that Mania is a condition acquired by nature, because I suspect it is acquired by nurture, by which I mean personal experience. I tend to focus on any challenge and suffer from being obsessive and compulsive. I have no doubt my father played an important role in my condition, which I have learned to control particularly with people, who may be intimidated by my obsessive focus.

One of the great lessons of my life has been that, (excluding Grace) nothing of value I have ever achieved could have succeeded without focus and intense passion, which is the Codex Canonical I have passed to my children, and grandchildren:

"The extra mile is the least populated"

The most dangerous and incomprehensible example of obsessive love, which for hundreds of years has never been addressed and probably never will be, is the love of a soldier for his country, his comrades, and his God. This Mania, or obsession, in the military is highly infectious and ensures that a soldier facing immense dangers fights with his heart. He will ignore his head when ordered to advance or defend a position, where he is most certain to die, and there comes a point in the process, when he wants to die. This is the kind of military training to which I and hundreds of thousands of other young men over hundreds of years have been exposed after being trained for military service.

The consequence is a type of Mania or obsession because the first part of military training is to develop in highly impressionable young soldiers an obsession to hate your enemy, and a passion to wish to kill them, while at the same time to love God, and love your country, and your comrades with the same passion, and a commitment to be prepared to die for them.

This is the point at which the seeds of post-traumatic stress disorder (PTSD) are sown because the young and very impressionable soldier has been stripped of all personal identity, his civilian clothes are removed, and he is forced to wear a uniform and badge of an adopted new family. He has imposed upon his impressionable young mind the positive philosophy of loving his God and country. He will attend a compulsory Sunday morning church parade where a theologically trained army officer, wearing a religious dog-collar explains God's part of the plan, which usually avoids his congregation being trained to kill. Neither is it explained that often only hundreds of yards away a foreign enemy is being told the same story, by their spiritual leaders.

These doctrines are irreconcilable, love and hate cannot unite because they are dissimilar frequencies, both require the fuel of competing passion. The opposite to love is not hate it is indifference, just ignore love and it will die.

Oliver Cromwell was the primary architect of the structure of military Mania when, after failing to win the first battle of the civil war in Edge Hill between the towns of Banbury and Warwick, in the UK he addressed his troops, saying:

"I only want soldiers to fight, who have the heart of the matter in them"

The poet John Milton saw that it was Cromwell's heart, and not an irrational intellectual analysis to die, which created the Mania and why he was ready to die for his country, and his God, with soldiers who wanted only to follow Cromwell to his death. Describing the attributes of Cromwell's heart, the poet Milton said of him:

"He was guided by faith and matchless fortitude, but first of all acquired the government of himself, and over himself won his greatest victories"

However, the heart is an unreliable organ, and emotions make unreliable masters because on September the 11th 1649, Cromwell lead 12,000 men and heavy 48 pounder guns in battering the town of Drogheda in Ireland into submission, killing 2,000 men, women and children, in addition to murdering hundreds of prisoners who had surrendered before the battle began. This dark tragedy was followed by the siege of Wexford where over 2,000 men women and children were also slaughtered.

After the battles, Cromwell wrote a letter to the speaker of the House of Commons for the British Parliament, and here is a sentence from the letter, in which he attempts to defend his actions:

> *"I am persuaded that this was a righteous judgement of God on these barbarous wretches who have dipped their hands in innocent blood"*

However, the very heavy price we pay for destroying the lives of others is the destruction of our own life. This is the challenge of military personnel attempting to return to normal life with some form of post-traumatic stress disorder, hating their enemy, but with conflicting love for their God and country.

Cromwell is the most hated man in the long painful history of Ireland, but he was no exception to the PTSD trauma because, after the war, he suffered long periods of isolation and depression, but it did not end there. On the 30th of January 1661, twelve years after he authorized the execution of King Charles the first, Cromwell's body was exhumed from Westminster Abbey, taken to Tyburn, and hung in chains for months before being thrown into a garbage pit.

Accepting that Mania is a form of both the love and hatred that can flow from mental illness, we do not have to look beyond the battle of the Somme for an example of the greatest example of love, Mania, or obsession, and the collective insanity of the British Military. This battle began on July the first, 1916 and by the end of daylight on the first day, twenty thousand teenaged British soldiers had been slaughtered, before they had begun to live. They died because they were told by their officers to run towards the machine guns of the enemy, carrying only a single shot rifle, or handgun.

These brave British soldiers, obsessed with the philosophy of love and hatred imposed upon them, were described later by Field Marshall Montgomery as, *"lions led by donkeys."*

However, the same also applied to the Germany Army, as the lives of their young men were equally recklessly squandered. The battle ended four months later, on November the 18th, 1916 with over three hundred thousand young men dead, and over one million with life changing injuries. One of the wounded heroes of this battle, who did not die, was my own father, who lost his right arm and subsequently died much too young, in consequence to his severe life changing injuries. He would never discuss the battle, his severe injuries, or his close comrades, who just disappeared in their trenches filled with mud. He only ever described this fearful moment of history as living in hell.

In this insane battle, not an inch of ground was lost or gained, by either side. Military commanders chose to ignore the reality that obsessive love and hatred, developed by brain washing, has very serious long-term psychological consequences. Highly impressionable young soldiers had love and hate violently imposed upon them, the most vital but deeply opposed emotional philosophies of the human condition. Young soldiers are taught to passionately hate and passionately love at one and the same time, which is impossible, because hate and love are immensely powerful energies.

While emotionally very similar, these energies can never unite because they are diametrically opposed to each other, ensuing both energies will die, because nothing of value can be sustained or built whilst they are in conflict. Every retiring soldier has some form of post-traumatic stress disorder, which can manifest in many ways, such as low self-esteem, isolation, guilt, insomnia, impotence, and regular flashbacks to terrifying moments of their history. A vast number of young soldiers returning to civilian life cannot adjust to reuniting with a loving partner, because of haunting memories of comrades who did not return, and the people whose lives they destroyed. Their dark memories are now appearing as living portraits in their dreams, or on their bedroom walls, which no loving wife can compete with, or possibly understand.

It is further validated by the strong fraternal bond which exists between all ex-servicemen, whatever rank, or regiment. The veteran will never forget his military number or cease to weep with other veterans on a Memorial Day but will never discus his tears because the pain is unbearable, and the cross of retrospection far too heavy to carry.

Attempting to understand love is a massive undertaking because there are so many parts which must be individually understood and, like pieces of a jig saw puzzle, carefully fitted together to create a most beautiful picture. The challenge with Mania is that it is an obsessive passion, like a mutating cell upon which nothing can be built or grown, or be sustained, because it feeds upon itself, and ultimately self-destructs.

After only twenty years of peace since World War one, in September 1939 war was declared again by the German people, who were passionately in love with their leader, and many shared a common hatred of the Jewish people. During four years of war, seventy-five million people needlessly died, and six million Jews were deported on an industrial scale, and systematically murdered. This involved thousands of ordinary people hunting for Jews in every occupied European country and required a massive logistical infrastructure to transport by rail in cattle wagons six million innocent people, just because they were Jewish. These innocent victims of Nazi Mania from all over Europe were stripped of every possession, and gassed and cremated with their children, with no survivors to mourn their passing.

A worrying sign of Mania can be seen in the growth of fundamentalism in Islam, which now has over one billion communicants. This should not be a problem, as Islam at its root is a peaceful religion, but Islam has a militant military arm which is growing exponentially, attracting young men from countries at war with America and Britain. It was seen as surrender and cowardice when we walked off the battlefield in both Iraq and Afghanistan, and left countries destroyed by our aggression. The Islamic militant recruitment program targets the latent but immense potential of love in Mania, and this emotional strategy is highly effective, because it requires serious disciples where the "heart of the matter must be in them."

The trainee terrorist must adopt a theological sub-frame which is to learn and adopt the five pillars of Islam and reconcile the irreconcilable philosophies of hating all non-Muslims, and loving their prophet, Mohamed, at the same time.

The Five Pillars of Islam Profession of Islamic Faith
Prayer five times every day
Alms to the poor
Fasting
Pilgrimage to Mecca

Obsession of any kind can be dangerous, and praying five times every day may create obsessive Mania and perhaps some form of mental illness. How else could it be possible to persuade any intelligent young person to strap dynamite around their body, before walking into a crowded area, and detonating an explosive device, killing many innocent people? Without Mania, or obsessive love, it would be impossible.

Some years ago, I was negotiating a contract in an important business meeting, when my visitor suddenly asked if he could be excused because he needed to pray. I have spent most of my life negotiating, and I am familiar with the tactic of diversionary stimulus, which diverts an opponent's attention by making an emotionally stimulating enquiry blunting his objectivity, such as, *"Do you have children,"* or *"do you play golf?"* They are highly emotive questions, designed to divert. He returned after ten minutes from an adjacent room and, pointing to his telephone, said my phone reminds me when it's time to pray, and we continued with our business, which we completed. He was always honorable, but the love he had for God and prayer might be considered as obsessive because it transcended our business.

As we bring this chapter on Mania to a close, we see, hidden behind the masquerade of love, the immense potential danger of obsession. Mania is like a form of nuclear energy that can be channeled by human will to create great value for humankind, or incalculable destruction. If there is a greater example of Mania than a young person wearing a suicide vest, I cannot imagine what it is.

However, the subtle and great danger of Mania is transcended by the much greater danger of Ludus, or flirting love, which can leave in its wake the most devastating and irreversible consequences of psychological damage to children, or fraud on a massive scale for vulnerable adults, flirting with their emotions and playing a game, with the secret mysteries of love.

Chapter 9

LUDUS AND FLIRTING LOVE

"She loved me for the dangers that had passed, and I loved her that she did pity me, this is the only witchcraft I have used" (William Shakespeare)

"If we love one another, God dwells in us" (1 John 4:12)

"Love must be understood backward but lived forward" (Kierkegaard)

Flirting may be an important part of love, and often a proper response to a perception of value, because it is often the place where a love affair begins, after we first notice something that we think is valuable or attractive in another person. This is where we mentally decide to allow a relationship to develop naturally, or help it along a little, or even let it pass, but often the place where we bury our common sense beneath the unreliable influence of our heart.

On one hand flirting can be one of the most exciting and innocent dimensions of emerging love, because it requires an open heart, which is vulnerable and defenseless. However, like Mania, it is potentially one of the most dangerous dimensions of a loving experience because it may be a little flame which you are confident you can control, until it consumes us and burns others we love. It is powerful because love is the most powerful energy of all human emotions, which can create great joy, but if misused or defiled it can destroy our equilibrium and peace in seconds, and the consequences can last a lifetime. The only way to avoid spilling our most powerful energy and damaging others is for us to become love ourselves, and love must become who we really are, and not an adopted persona, to play the game of love.

"We are who we are in our excellence, it is not an act, it is a habit" (Plato)

The challenge is that flirting may appear to be innocent fun, but because we are tampering with our emotions it may have the most devastating emotional and psychological consequences for us. Flirting should be allowed to develop with great care, because as it develops it may become obsessive and difficult to abandon or control, with the dreadful consequences of broken marriages and the happiness of children. Flirting used to be a popular dynamic of office work, because loving our job and our colleagues creates unity and a more efficient and productive working environment. The staff in a well-run office often become a kind of family because where unity in any group of focused hearts and minds exist, there is always much greater spiritual energy.

"The whole is greater than the sum of its parts" (Aristotle)

Many successful relationships leading to marriages developed in consequence to office flirting that then progressed into a serious relationship.

However, many marriages have been destroyed when flirting at one office Christmas party grew into a serious illicit love affair. This concern may not be a challenge in the future because any gender related observation or comment in a workplace may now be illegal.

The challenge young lovers have is, if love develops as a proper response to a perception of value, how do we share the value we have perceived? If a young man says, "I love your dress," or a girl says, "I love your tie," are they breaking the law by indicating gender pressure or emotional interest? However, whilst the dynamics of the workplace have changed, and flirting may now be technically illegal, the dynamics of internet flirting have exploded beyond anything we could have imagined.

Whilst the internet has unimaginable opportunities, it has comparable dangers in most western countries. This is fueled by the development of the phenomena of the dating Apps or Websites which are growing exponentially. According to Action Fraud, the National Fraud and Cyber Centre, many women who begin flirting by dating online are subsequently defrauded. Research carried out by the banking Industry found that a quarter of dating website users had been scammed during the last year for a total of 7.9 million pounds with an average loss of £321. However, the most worrying part of this story is that the number of frauds had increased by 50% over the previous year.

The paradigm for instant relationships has clearly changed as in 2020, dating apps in the UK were used 2.3 million times, by people looking for romance. Historically, before social media, flirting became the most effective and secure way to fall in love after seeing qualities in another person and wanting those values for yourself. The danger with flirting online is if there is no actual meeting there is no value which can be validated, whilst at the same time many evils can be fabricated and disguised. What transpires is the people talking about a loving relationship online are not falling in love with a human being, they are falling in love with the dream and illusion of a counterfeited loving relationship, which can never exist between the parties talking to each via a keyboard.

In the UK, 46% of marriages end in divorce and there are over 100,000 single women, with an average age of thirty-eight, being released back into the prospective marriage market in the UK every year. Many of these ladies are hungrily searching for romance previously denied, neglected, or destroyed by them or their husband. They may be a little too anxious, ensuring that they will quickly revisit their previous mistakes.

However, their target partner is in many cases playing the long game and has become an expert in listening to women anxious to talk about themselves. The seducer makes notes during these monologues and then tells his victims exactly what they want to hear. He loves opera, poetry, children, and sunsets but cannot meet for two months because he is finishing a contract on an oil rig. However, notwithstanding this set-back he would like to continue to talk and share, until they are able to meet in the restaurant near to her home, which she is asked to reserve, together with a room at a local five-star hotel.

In the two months before the meeting, he talks to her every other day, often in the most intimate and personal terms, and she quickly comes to believe she is in love because they have so many similar hopes and aspirations. The week before the meeting he tells her he is in dispute with his oil company, and his money will not be released until the last day of his contract. Whilst he can wait before meeting her, he hates doing so, and if she is able to transfer to him £1,800 for the flight and hotel, he will re-pay her immediately they meet because his contract will have been cleared.

Hopelessly in love with a self-created illusion of love, and the opportunity to meet the man of her dreams very soon, she happily sends the money to a bank in some distant country, and the love she so desperately hoped for disappears, never to be heard from again.

Perhaps a little wiser she joins the millions of other lonely women floating in cyber-space trying to forget, not only the cruel deception and expensive consequences, but her broken heart, which because of fear she may never repair. In 2020 over one hundred and fifty million pounds was stolen online from lonely women, desperate for romance. It has become the biggest growth sector in the history of crime.

However, there is another side to flirting which is far more sinister than corrupted love and more dangerous, and that is grooming children for criminal abuse, stealing their most precious resource which is their innocence. In a recent report from Children's Charities, some two hundred thousand children have been approached, and many abused.

We therefore have Ludus or flirting, as an aspect of love which cannot be ignored because it is part of the whole experience of love, and it can grow into something of immense beauty. It may also destroy young lives which are emotionally unable to deal with the shame or guilt of being groomed and may self-harm for punishment, to validate their false perception of low self-esteem. This therefore means that it is going to be much harder for parents to raise children in a loving and secure environment, when through the internet and social media children have immediate access to people and information which may disturb them emotionally or irreversibly damage their lives.

A young person suffering from low self-esteem is dangerously vulnerable to the illusion of love created by the appearance of counterfeit love. This seductive flirting may persuade the young victim that they possess value and deserved to be loved, which may be achieved by flirting or flattery. Parents of children having access to the internet, which today includes virtually every child, must assume their inquisitive children are exposed to flirting with unacceptable people or material because an insatiable appetite for new information is the beauty and essence of a healthy child. This dimension of anxious parenting was unknown to previous generations, but it is now essential for parents to maintain a much closer instinctive resonance by listening more to their child, because children cannot continuously keep a secret or effectively disguise what is in their hearts, but we will never hear if we remain too busy to listen.

The final danger of flirting is what has become known as "Catfishing" which is where the perpetrator searches the internet to find a woman who he perceives to be vulnerable and slowly begins to control and emotionally manipulate her. This is not to defraud her or seduce her but relieve his own boredom by enjoying influencing her life and her family responsibilities.

This is a flirting game enjoyed by married men who are under the control of their own wives and have no wish for an extra-marital relationship, but who want to enjoy the illusion of an intimate relationship by controlling a woman, and so they tell their victim everything she needs to capture her confidence. This illusion of a relationship may last for a long time because neither party want it to end, but it can be psychologically damaging if the truth of a false persona emerges. In the meantime, while a loving dialogue may satisfy the psychological need to love and be loved by both parties, it also diverts love from their own families who should be the sole beneficiaries of their affection.

Perhaps, more so for a woman, the passion to love can quickly become a passion of hate, which was cleverly summed up in clear text by William Congreve, when he said:

"Heaven has no rage like love to hatred turned or hell no fury like a woman scorned"

Juxtaposed to this experience is the statement by Juliet in Shakespeare's Romeo and Juliet, when separating from her lover Romeo, she said:

"Parting is such sweet sorrow"

The challenge that intimate partners have when deciding to part is, whether they are aware of it or not, the irreconcilable passions of love and hate become trapped in the spiritual battlefield of their hearts. Some days they might experience an overwhelming love for their partner and other days they might wish they were dead.

The love-hate phenomena rapidly accelerates as the partners begin to push each other physically, emotionally, and psychologically to their limits of sanity, while the stronger one often becomes stronger, and the weaker one becomes weaker or more withdrawn and more subdued.

This incomprehensible experience is that quite often in some curious psycho-sexual way their love and hatred merge and the whole experience becomes uncontrollably larger as they progress in this cycle of devastation and mutual self-destruction. There would seem to be no credible reason why a woman would choose to continue in an abusive relationship. People outside the relationship cannot comprehend an abused person waiting outside the prison to be reunited with their abuser who was imprisoned for spousal abuse.

The World Health Organization reported that with women between the ages of sixteen to sixty, one in three have been subjected to physical or sexual violence with an intimate partner. If these published numbers are only half accurate, women have a massive health problem, and we are witnessing a global pandemic of femicide. On average, the police in England and Wales receive over one hundred calls an hour relating to domestic violence according to His Majesty's Inspectorate of Constabulary, (HMIC 20:15) but only 18% of women suffering abuse from an intimate partner report the offence.

The statistics are staggering and so the serious question this poses for us is how we can prepare our young daughters for the hatred and violence lying disguised and dormant in far too many relationships, and how can they be released from the incarceration of a diseased union.

Education is the best way to prepare young women and young men and even older people to understand the signs causing concern. Also, we need to understand what is hoped for in a relationship and have our "must haves" and "can't stands" list prior to even going on that first date, because choosing happiness is a personal decision. Most people even on their best behavior will provide subtle signs and we can see the red flags within the first few dates, if we are watching and are sensitive to signals. Unfortunately, there are some truly evil people in the world today and I'm not sure there is any hope for them. However, most are just very selfish and insecure which causes them to lash out, and take their frustrations out on those closest to them. They can be helped but not by the person often closest to them, it must be by an outside force, either a counsellor or by the love found in God who can change even the worst criminal's heart.

Unfortunately, we cannot protect those who don't want protection or don't even know that they are in an abnormal relationship. If they are not willing to remove themselves from the situation to get help and allow their abuser to get help, then there is no hope for that relationship, and it will proceed to violence until they part, or one of them is dead.

However, in addition to protecting women we should be investing more energy in understanding the psycho/sexual dimensions of a relationship. These often begin passionately and harmoniously but slowly decline from verbal to physical abuse. Curiously notwithstanding the abuse, the partners often wish to continue the relationship until the abuse becomes unbearable, or one of the partners is injured or dead.

We need to invest more of our time and energy in healthy relationships such as Agape, the gold standard of love in which each partner abandons self-interest and cares for the other's wellbeing in the same way God's love is manifested in Jesus Christ's sacrifice for us. We need to understand our true value, and so not be tempted to enter a dysfunctional relationship because of our low self-esteem.

It is far better to remain single than to enter a relationship you cannot break with someone who has latent anger or strong self-interests, which you mistakenly believe you can change.

People do not easily change, who they really are and whilst they may disguise their true character, it will be manifest in their relationship with their parents, family, and friends. Any signs of indifference or unforgiving selfishness must be the signal to immediately terminate the relationship because character defects are the routes of domestic abuse. Defects in the family life of others will become defects in your life, but why gamble with your future happiness, just because you think you need love today, when all you need is a little more self-awareness.

When the partner who once loved you is completely indifference to you, remember love and hate are comparable but irreconcilable intense passions of the heart and mind. This is a form of Mania when the delicate balance of the heart and mind is disturbed, and we see some form of mental illness, which can quickly become mentally and physically abusive.

The challenge that intimate angry partners have when deciding to part, is that neither of them really want to do so, and the irreconcilable passions of love and hate become trapped in the spiritual battlefield of their hearts. Some days you may want to love your partner as you have never loved, and some days you could think of nothing more grotesque.

This love hatred phenomena rapidly accelerates with shouting and the partners begin to physically push each other with the stronger becoming stronger and the weaker becoming weaker. The incomprehensible experience is that quite often in some psycho/sexual way their love and hatred merge and becomes addictive until the relationship deteriorates.

The serious question this poses for us is how we can prepare our young women for the hatred and violence lying disguised and dormant in far too many relationships, and how they can be released from the incarceration of a diseased union. I cannot accept that men were born to be brutal, or women to be brutalized, or indeed that deeply loving another human being can fuel such fury, hate and violence, but the evidence exposes a massive failure in our culture to understand relationships and protect women.

Chapter 10

PHILAUTIA AND SELF LOVE

"Self- love, my liege is not so vile a sin as self-neglect." (William Shakespeare)

"If you love yourself, you will have no rivals." (Benjamin Franklin)

"No man is free who is not the master of himself." (Epictetus)

"He first of all acquired the government of himself." (Milton)

Freedom of choice is the most valuable attribute of being human because it enables us to reinvent ourselves and choose happiness whenever the life we have chosen has become unattractive and unacceptable. Life is far too short to endure a relationship which is not expanding, and therefore slowly dying.

The first thing we need to understand is that self-love is not possible, because love must be a bi-lateral experience or it is not love, but only disguised self-interest. Love requires two entities, a benefactor and beneficiary who play equal and opposite reversable roles in this game of hearts rehearsed and played in most intimate of circumstances. Only consider change if the roles are inequal and cannot be re-balanced but remember the wisdom of the philosophers advising on the recourses you will need.

"The trial you face, will introduce you to your strengths" Epictetus

"Fear not, I am your strength and exceeding great reward" (Genesis 15:1)

"He must increase, and I must decrease" (John 3:30)

Re-inventing ourselves needs very careful but brutally honest recollection, because to quote the tribal wisdom of my mother, we can easily jump from the frying pan into the fire, or if we are lost walking in a forest or sailing on an ocean and decide to change direction, we will still be lost.

The first challenge we face is to understand just how we arrived at where are, and accept the responsibility, avoiding blaming others for our own poor choices. Self-love is a thief, because behind the smile there is a vacuous heart which is driven by self-interest. It is fueled, and continuously re-filled by energy drained from the loving resources of everyone they meet, leaving their benefactors feeling reduced and bereft of love or energy.

This is difficult to understand because it is impossible for us to form an objective and accurate opinion of ourselves when we carry around so many different personas or masks, and the real question we must answer before we decide to change and reinvent ourselves is, who am I?

This was the most difficult philosophical question ever to challenge the human intellect, identified by Socrates, (350 BC) perhaps the wisest of all the Greek philosophers who allegedly saw this, inscribed on the tomb of Apollo.

"Know yourself"

This is the most important question of all time, because if you are not sure of who you really are and fail to accurately acknowledge your experience, fears, and aspirations, until you are sure you must not build plans to change your life.

This most important question for all humanity was asked of God by the great Jewish King David, who was the father of Solomon, the wisest man who ever lived. David was under the clearest galaxy in the Judean desert, four thousand years ago, which has been recorded for all time in the Bible. After King David considered the vast universe of the moon and stars, which ordained the earth, he realized how insignificant he was, and asked God.

What is man, that you are compulsively obsessed with him? (Psalm 8:4)

As we search our hearts, minds, and experience to face knowing ourselves, we need to think of every time we have put on a brave face, when we felt everything but brave, because it is a collection of theses faces or diverse personas, which will impede our search for our true selves, which is often less attractive than who we dream of becoming.

A *"persona"* is a sound passing through a hole in a mask which was used to disguise or change identities, when used by actors in Greek tragedies to play different kinds of people, whilst wearing different kinds of masks and creating different sounds.

Most people carry different personas which may be professional, domestic, or religious masks, but are all different and we may be guilty of selecting the most suitable persona or mask for important meetings, or relationships. However, the longer or more often we wear the mask the heavier it will be to carry, and it will one day fall from our face, when the sad, under-developed person behind the mask will be exposed.

The biggest challenge we have, when we are attempting to appear as someone we are not, is that we are stealing from ourselves the opportunity to expose and develop our true value, and as love is a proper response to a perception of value, we are missing the opportunity of falling in love.

A successful international businessman I knew who travelled a great deal in his business, died suddenly at sixty years of age, and at his funeral another unknown, additional, wife arrived, with two teenaged children.

It was obviously a long-term additional marriage involving the same man, but with two entirely different personas, which he required to maintain two different families, and I was reminded of the following warning:

"Who lives more life than one, more deaths than one must die" Oscar Wilde

Many people have been living more than one life for many years, by carrying around a range of different personas, and competing relationships such as professional, domestic, or even spiritual masks, pretending to be different people, or attempting to be all things to all men. However, living successful competing lives simultaneously is impossible and will ultimately be discovered, whilst seriously damaging to the psyche, and I am reminded of a Biblical text:

"A house divided against itself cannot stand" (Mark 3:25)

The problem we have managing two agendas simultaneously is that we are attempting to emotionally manage two conflicting frequencies, which is impossible without it seriously affecting our own physical health. Our spiritual balance is essential if we wish for sound physical health and often terminal illness will follow a serious emotional reversal.

The Scottish poet Robert Burns understood that we do not see ourselves as honestly as we should, and I am reminded of a line from one of his poems:

"Would some power the gift to give us, to see ourselves as others see us"

If we want to understand this aspect of self-love, we should look more closely at seeing ourselves as others see us, defining the word, "See" and defining the word, "Knowledge." See, as a noun, means the throne of a Pope or a Bishop; see as a verb, means much more than looking at ourselves, just using our eyes, we have many other choices of interpreting the world, leading to words such as insight, oversight, foresight, behold, perceive, observe, experience, inspect.

I fondly recall a man called Peter, a sight-less pianist in our church who greeted me every Sunday before I identified myself by saying, *"Great to see you, Norman."* This statement always puzzled me, but I never found the courage to discuss Peter's disability with him and what he meant when he said, "Great to see you, Norman," but it became clear to me we were seeing many different perspectives of the same thing, and looking at a single mirror on the wall was poor research for an important judgement.

A reflection of ourselves in a mirror will not reveal the kind of person we are if we attempt to emulate actors in a Greek tragedy, disguising our identity and projecting images of beauty by carrying many masks of different personas.

One of the biggest challenges I encountered in my professional life was, management burn-out, which is slowly being identified and recognized as male mid-life crisis. This occurs when the hopes and aspirations of talented young people are overtaken by the horrors of reality, and their corporate masks become too heavy to carry. These mid-life managers are often promoted to responsibilities beyond their skill set, and the heavy personas they have carried for years, slowly begin to implode.

The cost to the corporation of a broken-down executive is very high, but nothing compared with the cost to a family of a mentally ill husband and father. I recall the wisdom of Abraham Lincoln referring to the different masks people carry around when he said:

"You can fool all of the people some of the time, and some of the people all the time, but you cannot fool all of the people all the time"

The reality of endeavoring to disguise who we think we are, as exposed by Lincoln, is unsustainable because whatever our choice of persona, it becomes progressively heavier as we get older, and the facade slowly begins to implode. This reveals what the person behind the persona has become, which is a fearful, child-like figure in the corner of a room sucking a thumb in a fetal position, behind a lifetime of broken masks. The truth is that we are who we are, and not who we would like to be, because we cannot indefinitely maintain a damaged or disguised illusion of who we are pretending to be. In addition to seeing, we need the knowledge to understand what we are seeing.

The Greeks had several words for knowledge:

Gnosis	*Knowledge of fact; scientific knowledge, such as 2+2=4*
Gnosco	*Knowledge acquired by extensive education and experience.*
Epignosis	*Knowledge which is instinctive, beyond the senses, first-hand.*
Eido	*Knowledge where the knower and the knowledge become one*

Shakespeare makes the argument, **"Self-love is better than self-neglect,"** but self-love is counterfeited love and reflects where love has been swamped by self-interest. Narcissism is not self-love, it is self-neglect because it diverts us from merging the value we see in others with the value we see in ourselves, missing an opportunity to expand and share our love, and gain a richer experience.

Therefore, stand back and try to discover who you really are, what you have, and what you do not have, and build on what you have, choosing happiness and remember the wisdom of the poetry of John Donne, and reinvent yourself:

"Be your own castle, or the world will be your jail"

Chapter 11

PRAGMA AND ENDURING LOVE

"He is not a lover, who does not love forever." (Euripides)

Enduring love is the rarest form of love and the most difficult to obtain and sustain, because most young people who live together before marriage often do not really get to know each other until unattractive, unacceptable characteristics emerge, and the opportunity and patience to love and learn has disappeared from the relationship.

In the UK last year there were 242,000 marriages and 108,421 divorces, which statistics reveal that approaching 50% of all marriages in the UK end in tears. The question we perhaps should first address is why many of our own young people are incapable of securing a loving relationship, and what is happening to our children?

Our immediate reaction is to challenge the statement, *"loving for ever"* by Euripides, because it appears to be a simply philosophical concept and an impossible dream, which disqualifies us as enduring lovers. However, it is possible to love and be loved forever, as will be seen in the final chapter of this book, after we have examined the word Agape, which is unconditional love.

The very sad consequence of these horrific national statistics is that there are three million children in the UK witnessing the tragic reality that love is an illusion and does not exist for them, and therefore is perceived to never exist.

Nature has declared that two very different human beings are required to create a child, and it must follow that those two very different human beings are required to raise and equip the child for the many challenges of life. However, this becomes an impossible dream when the once loving passion of parents turns into the powerful passion of hate, often filled with the bitterness of losing love.

The position is much worse in the US, with 25% of all children under the age of 24 living with a single parent, which is three time higher than any other country in the world, and no great testimony to the quality of life in the greatest nation on earth. So, what has happened to the enduring state of love so revered by Euripides?

The answer is not complex, and Euripides can talk about love all day, but it will be meaningless until we not only comprehend, (understand) love but are able to be apprehended (arrested) by Love. To do this we must turn our pages back and remind ourselves of what we have already seen in this book.

Generosity is a prerequisite of unconditional love, and self-interests destroys the possibility of ever experiencing love because for the selfish person, love will always die.

Hidden in the incomprehensible mysteries of loving is the process of letting go, because to love we must let go of whatever we would like to retain. We should remember the wisdom of Aristotle in the second chapter of our book when he exposed loving and letting go, one of the greatest mysteries of life and love:

"The only love we keep is the love we give away"

It is not love, unless there is a reckless generosity in loving; as a sailor might throw away a compass, we must throw our self-interest away, and allow love to perform its miracle of unifying, because as the poet Byron writes:

"Love was born a twin and cannot grow in isolation"

Love is dynamic, it either grows or it dies. Any tiny part of ourselves we hold back for fear of rejection will grow exponentially and become a vast dark refuge for us until we succeed in starving our love to death and are left nursing a heart shaped vacuum in our soul.

I have great confidence in young people, but I tremble for their happiness because the culture of relationships has changed so radically since our parents married. Our culture in those days was, "not under my roof" and very few couples lived together, until they became friends and knew each other before falling in love, getting married, and living together, never thinking of divorce.

Today couples decide to live together weeks, or sometimes days after meeting, and invest little or no time in getting to know each other, which may create the illusion the couple have experienced some form of love. Regardless of age, both parties bring baggage to the party from previous relationships, which may not be discovered until the co-habitation matures.

Whilst the Eros experience may be memorable, it is likely to be transient and often disappears as quickly as it arrived, because in isolation, unsupported by the many other attributes of love, Eros as an experience of enduring love is simply not sustainable.

If we experience only Eros, or just a physical relationship as a part of love we miss the opportunity to build a relationship in all other essential aspects of loving until we discover the party is over and our partner, with whom we have little other interests, has moved on. This often leaves the small children of the unholy union weeping because they trusted love as an enduring entity, which has vanished, and often turned before their eyes to hate.

The simple indicator of whether a relationship we are considering has the quality upon which we can construct an enduring love affair, is, what is the level of generosity you perceive in your potential partner? There is nothing more important in building an enduring love affair than generosity and this is revealed in the tiniest events, which will indicate whether you come first or second in their thoughts, because generosity is the antithesis of self-interest.

Avoid a relationship where your potential partner does not love their family, because someone who does not love their mother is disconnected and barren, and someone who does not love their father will always be anti-authority and demand control of every part of your life, and the lives of your children.

These sad people will never be able to experience true or enduring love because love cannot be taught it can only be slowly grown by the experience of being loved. If this does not exist, it never will because love is never immobile it is dynamic and it must be fed, to expand, or it will lowly die through neglect. If love is not based on genuine growing friendship, it will not endure. If we are in a relationship where love is dead or dying and we want it renewed, and revitalized, we must endeavor to build a friendship in areas of special interest to our partner. If we are not prepared to invest in our partner's life, love has passed us by, and we are avoiding our hope of happiness.

Every valuable part of life including enduring relationships comes at a cost, which means abandoning self-interest and focusing all our thoughts and time on our partner. Love is the only way to change another person and our generosity which cannot be impeded it will invade their soul and transform their lives. If love is weaponized, there is no defense to its power or affect.

"A true sign of intelligence is not knowledge, but imagination" (Einstein)

However poorly disguised, there appears to be an eloquent cry in the word, Agape, for a reciprocation of the Grace and unconditional love we are given. The paradox appears to be that while we are loved unconditionally by God, we are expected to return the love in our worship, or it will die. However, it cannot die, because love will never die, it has no beginning or end, it simply fails to grow, often masquerading as a spiritual experience.

It is not possible to fully capture love until we fully understand that love at its most pure is a spiritual phenomenon in which sex may play no part. After an untold number of years circa 500 BC of attempting to define the purest love, which is unconditional, the word chosen by the theologians and consensus of wise men of Greece was, "Agape," which became the consolidated opinion of the great men of the day relating to human relationships primarily with God and each other.

Agape is one of the most powerfully eloquent words in any language because Agape defines a spiritual experience captured by abandoning self-interest and recklessly focussing our hearts and prayerful energies on the subject of our love. Abandoning self-interest guarantees our reckless unconditional love, will be strengthened and reciprocated.

Chapter 12

AGAPE

"Greater love has no man than this, that a man lay down his life for a friend" (John 15:13)

This is one of the greatest and most beautiful words in any language, which first appeared in Athens, circa 500 BC when the philosophers were searching for a word which encapsulated the secret of true and lasting beauty. After endless debates the consensus of the symposia's decided it could be only achieved when we individually decided to change and forgive all transgressions created against and by us, and we unconditionally loved everyone we met, and everything we do. Although it was accepted that such a high quality of spiritual life would be beyond the reach of even the most righteous individuals, it was also accepted as the highest level to which any human being, searching for beauty could aspire.

However, the word Agape appears paradoxical and curiously reciprocal because Agape asks for nothing in return for the unconditional love God provides for us, and there are no reciprocal conditions attached to God's gift of love to us. However, because love requires a flow and contra-flow of spiritual energy between two separate entities, God requires prayer to validate and return to Him, the unconditional love He continually provides for us. Loving and being loved unconditionally is the highest point any truly enlightened couple could reach because, as Plato says:

"Love is a serious disease"

Whilst it is possibly to technically understand the Greek word, Agape, which is unconditional love, it is virtually impossible for us to apply the principles of unconditionally forgiving every betrayal or unkind experience we suffer because, while God forgives and forgets, humans may forgive, but never forget.

I have a friend who is a senior Banker, who had a brief affair with his secretary, which he quickly deeply regretted and terminated, but as he felt so guilty, he had to tell his wife, because he was sure she would forgive him. He transferred the joint property to her, and she did forgive him, and they were reconciled, and they have a lovely marriage. However, years later when they are alone together quietly watching television, and infidelity appears as part of what they are watching, he still feels unable to respond whilst his wife is looking at him, and he is sure she is remembering his betrayal.

This eloquent psychological scar has become a self-inflicted symbol of punishment and an indelible silent witness on the walls of his home, and he questions his judgment in confessing his betrayal of love. It would therefore appear that whilst we can forgive a betrayal of love, we can never forget because while the wound may heal, an eloquent residual scar may remain, and become a permanent cloud on an otherwise beautiful relationship.

As I bring this book to a close, I pose only one questions to myself. If love needs to unite to expand, how can I experience expanding love if I am living alone, and my wife, children or husband are gone?

The answer is to recognize that the problem is spiritual, so go and sit in the back of a church and thank God for loving you and ask God to receive the love you have been holding back and guide you to donate this love to others. You will hear from God very soon, because He has been waiting for a while to hear from you, and the circumstances of your first meeting with God will validate their authenticity.

However, there is no logic or intellectual structure in my response to these very important questions; my only recourse is to give to you my own life transforming experience of Agape, or love without conditions. This is my testimony:

I was 18 years of age in Italy, conscripted into the British Military Police. After winning the war, the British were an occupying army, much to the distress of the Italian people who were angered because our control and presence meant they had lost the war, and were subject to foreign occupation and military law, over which the Military Police had absolute control. I was surprised to be selected and trained as a Military Policeman, until I later observed that most of my colleagues were similarly uneducated, aggressive young men, with learning difficulties, of average intelligence, from dysfunctional families who could be brainwashed and sold a better life in the Military. We were given immense personal authority and power over civilian and military personnel in an occupied country, having been persuaded we were serving our God and country.

Many of the Italian young men were unemployed, demobilized ex-soldiers, who enjoyed provoking and assaulting British soldiers. Their girlfriends often took a British soldier into a dark alley, where her brothers waited to beat and rob him. Our task as Military Policemen was to arrest and prosecute the perpetrators of crimes against British soldiers and crimes committed by British soldiers, such as murder, arson, or rape, because soldiers commit the same crimes as civilians.

Seeking information from suspects of serious crimes always involves some form of questioning or interrogation, which can vary in the military, depending upon the nature of the crime. It is, as Friedrich Nietzsche (not my favorite German philosopher) said:

> *"If you stare into darkness long enough, you will also become dark"*

This progressively happened to me. During interrogations we were continually smoking, and I would regularly see two of my cigarettes burning in an ashtray at the same time. I was also drinking heavily and eating badly, hardly sleeping, and both my physical and mental health were deteriorating. My deterioration was juxtaposed to many of my Police colleagues, who became stronger and more confident, feeding and growing more powerfully in the trauma they inflicted on the suspects of their arrest and interrogation.

A phenomenon of power is that it corrupts everyone it infects and because interrogators investigate darkness, they become dark themselves; they can also smell fear in a guilty person, which fear is not present when interrogating an innocent man. When guilt is sensed by the interrogating policeman with his acquired dark instincts from a dysfunctional background, he is seldom wrong. All that is now required is a confession to close the case, and move on. At this point the interview often accelerates and deteriorates.

I am still haunted by the memory of these eighteen-year-old conscripted Military Policemen, many of whom, like me, had never had a girlfriend and had recently left their home and mother for the first time, not to join the Gestapo, but the British Army, to serve the Crown and country, but now suffering from a deterioration in their mental and moral health, as I was. I have never spoken of my experience as an 18-year-old, but the following is a brief memory of my decline in just in a few months from my mother's care into a level of insanity from which after 70 years I still get detailed flashbacks. I therefore write in an attempt to understand, because I have never understood, and the following is my attempt to rationalize a thesis of my very stressful experience, when I believed I was serving my country.

"The soul becomes dyed with the color of its thoughts" (Marcus Aurelius)

Once a questioner has convinced himself he is serving his God and country, from a higher level of humanity than his victim, he becomes intellectually and emotionally detached, because the questioner is no longer dealing with someone of his own quality, to whom he can relate, but a sub-human who has little or no value.

Our military responsibilities meant we were short-staffed and therefore on standby duty every night, spending our time playing snooker, drinking and smoking in the canteen waiting with our partner until we would be called to some accident or disturbance, usually British soldiers fighting each other or local youths. If a Policeman was injured after an incident, we would either go to the minor injury's unit at the military hospital or return to our barracks with our uniforms torn and suffering some injury, often more drunk than the soldiers we arrested.

One such evening two teams returned from a much bigger incident really torn and beaten up, and as was the custom the whole room began to cheer, because the more beaten up the returning team, the greater would be the cheers. When the noise had subsided someone shouted, *"Sing us a hymn, Hudson,"* followed by cheers. An eighteen-year-old returning policeman I didn't know, with a bandage around his head through which some blood had seeped, climbed on a table and began to sing a hymn, "Everyone ought to know who Jesus is," to a room which fell silent, followed by cheers and clapping when Hudson finished.

I was so messed up with what I was doing with my life and the general condition of my health, the following day I went to find Hudson, the policeman who had sung a hymn the previous evening. I asked him how he found the courage to sing a hymn to such an insane bunch of young potential psychopaths.

He told me he had little personal courage because, unlike some of the head-cases amongst us, he didn't enjoy hurting or getting hurt, and any courage I thought he possessed was not his but came from God, to whom he had committed his life. I asked him how I could find the courage he had found, and he suggested I become a Christian and he introduced me to a life of faith, which at the time was the greatest strength for me, because I was in the darkest place.

Without an adequate level of scholarship, or knowledge of theology to understand the full ramifications of faith, I learned that the Bible is a love story of reconciliation. It is where we experience a personal relationship with God and receive a clean sheet when everything from our mis-spent youth is not only forgiven, but more importantly it is forgotten. This means there are no eloquent scars on our history to remind and condemn us for who we used to be. If I were reading this story, I would suspect that the writer had dodged a bullet and escaped the consequence of his crimes and conveniently become religious, because this is what my army buddies thought of me. However, after 70 years of Christian life I still profoundly believe that a life built on love and faith is the only way to build a happy and enduring relationship. I recall the wisdom of Socrates:

> *"Happiness is not found in seeking more, but wanting less"*

I learned that coming to faith meant accepting the total depravity of mankind, the authority of the Bible, with the unlimited grace of the sovereignty of God. The change in my life was slow, because although I could intellectually accept that I had been forgiven by God, I could not accept that God had forgotten the crimes I had committed, because often I couldn't sleep. I was still suffering badly when I left the Army and returned to the love and care of my home, and my mother. After a period of serious disorientation, I decided to try to find a church and perhaps also find another "Hudson," who I badly missed, and I remembered the wisdom of the 13th century Islamic scholar, Rumi:

> *"Continue breaking your heart until it opens"*

After several disappointments, I found a church where I was warmly welcomed and I met Carol a lovely sixteen-year-old girl but, because of her studies and extensive further education, our relationship was limited to sitting together in church services, on Sunday morning.

I did not fall in love with Carol at first sight, I fell in love with her sense of humor, her faith, spiritual life, and personal peace, which I badly needed and wanted for myself. I instinctively knew that peace of mind was at the center of my recovery from the mental and psychological illness of PTSD bequeathed to me by the conflicting philosophies of love and hate imposed upon me during my military service to my beloved country.

Carol and I were married four years later when she had finished her education, and we have had sixty-five wonderful years together with our large and expanding family.

I close this simple offering with the words of Socrates one of the greatest minds of our long history who said:

"An unexamined life, is not worth living"

I remind myself of the simple framework of love: *Love is a proper response to a perception of value. God is love, and wherever love is manifest, God is always present. If love is not built on deeply growing friendship, it will never flower. Always be generous because self-interest is the enemy of love. Love is dynamic and will either grow or die, it is never stationary. Love must unite to expand, to become larger than the sum of its parts. The only way to weaponize your heart is to love your target more tomorrow than today.*

"Love makes everyone a poet" (Plato)

I confess I have written this book not to be understood, but to understand some of the deeper mysteries of loving and being loved, which I profoundly believe is the greatest secret to capturing great happiness and success in life. I would like to finish with the wisdom and experience of the Apostle Paul who was executed over two thousand years ago, because he is one of the greatest men who ever lived. He wrote the following statement on love, the finest I have ever heard, in his first letter to the church in Corinth recorded in the Bible, **(1 Corinthians 13:3)** to remind us of the challenges we face in seeking to love and be loved:

"Love suffers and is kind. Love does not envy. Love does not vaunt itself. Love is not puffed up. Love does not behave itself unseemly. Love seeks not her own. Love is not easily provoked. Love thinks no evil."

I would also ask you to consider the consequence of being loved by your children and at some distant time, their children, and your influence as a role model, in their lives, and I quote from the Bible.

"I have set before you, life and death, blessing and cursing, therefore choose life, that you, and your children may live" (Deuteronomy 30:19)

Over one billion Christians in the world have a relationship with God and have experienced that God is love and this simply cannot be a coincidence. This incalculable power of love is graciously offered without cost to us other than an obligation to pass on the love we receive to others. The secret mystery we cannot understand is that we are not the origin and source of love, nor are we a vault in a Bank to secure love. We are only channels of the love we receive and pass on, mysteriously enjoying the legacy of residual energy as the love passes through us.

This may be the end of my story, but not the end of love, because love will always be available for us as it is endless, and God may have been waiting a long time to hear from us.

"The love we give away, is the only love we keep."

Copyright 2024 Norman Gidney

Printed in Great Britain
by Amazon